Ending Poverty
A Basic Income for All Canadians

François Blais

Translated by Jennifer Hutchison

James Lorimer & Company, Publishers
Toronto, 2002

Originally published as *Un revenu garanti pour tous*

Copyright ©2001 Les Éditions du Boréal

Translation copyright ©2002 Jennifer Hutchison

All rights reserved. No part of this book may be reproduced or transmitted in any form or by any means, electronic or mechanical, including photocopying, or by any information storage or retrieval system, without permission in writing.

James Lorimer & Company Ltd. acknowledges the support of the Ontario Arts Council. We acknowledge the support of the Government of Canada through the Book Publishing Industry Development Program (BPIDP) for our publishing activities. We acknowledge the support of the Canada Council for the Arts for our publishing program.

National Library of Canada Cataloguing in Publication Data

Blais, François
    Ending poverty: a basic income for all Canadians

Translation of: Un revenu garanti pour tous.
Includes index.
ISBN 1-55028-755-9

1. Guaranteed annual income—Canada. I. Hutchison, Jennifer. II. Title.

HD4928.A5B213 2002   362.'82   C2002-900315-6

James Lorimer & Company Ltd., Publishers
35 Britain Street
Toronto, Ontario
M5A 1R7
www.lorimer.ca

Printed in Canada

To Laurence, Camille and Paul, to help them understand that justice is one of the greatest objectives that we can pursue and to the memory of their grandfather, Jacques Morisset.

Table of Contents

Foreword — viii

Foreword to the French Edition — xi

Acknowledgements — xiii

Introduction — xiv

Chapter 1
Waging War Against Poverty Instead of the Poor — 1
Essential background — 1
A Basic Income or Guaranteed Annual Income? — 3
   A few examples of possible names — 3
   The unconditionality feature — 5
Understanding poverty in industrialized nations — 7
   "Non-working" poor — 7
   "Working" poor — 8
Fighting against exclusion without increasing poverty — 9
   Giving more to the jobless? — 10
   Increasing the minimum wage? — 11
   Avoiding the situation of favouring one group over the other — 12
Poverty and unemployment traps — 12
   When it is more worthwhile to do nothing than to work — 13
   When living with one or more people only makes things worse — 14
   Deconstructing a culture of poverty — 14
Another route to take: Basic Income — 15
   Fighting the unemployment trap while avoiding workfare — 15
   Finding a different way of "taxing" the poor — 16
   Improving opportunities for job holders — 17
   Finding a more distributive structure that is better for non-workers — 18

Chapter 2
Reconciling Efficiency and Fairness in a Changing World 21
Two values not to be separated: efficiency and justice 21
   Efficiency and justice do not need to compete with one another 22
   Attempting to define these two values 23
   "Everyone according to their worth" is not an acceptable standard 25
   What kind of equality are we looking for? 27
The economic role of social policies 28
   Limits of market mechanisms 28
   What the government can do to help the economy 30
   The place for income security in a healthy economy 31
   Challenging the welfare state 33
New constraints of a changing world 33
   The first steps made by the contemporary welfare state 34
   The end of this model 35
   Victims of the "new economy" 36
Economic grounds for a Basic Income 37
   Ease of administration and transparency of transfers 38
   Less bureaucracy and more financial security 40
   Where everyone has the same advantages in working 41
   Supporting poorly paid activities 42
   More flexibility in work organization 44
   What will happen to the minimum wage? 44
   And what about other salaries? 45
   Diversifying incomes rather than focusing completely on work 46
A Basic Income and social justice 48
   Putting a Basic Income in an intellectual and political context 48
   Giving to everyone, including the "lazy"? 49
   Inequality of opportunities and circumstances 51
   Redistributing wealth while respecting dignity 53
   The priority of the right to income over the right to work 54
   Increasing opportunities for those who have the least 58

Chapter 3
Achieving a Basic Income Starting Now 64
The challenges of change 64
Preliminary thoughts on costs 65
   A look at two complementary notions 66
   Why does a Basic Income cost more? 67
Various funding options to explore 69

Relying on an increase of business activity and on savings generated by simplifying bureaucracy	70
Giving only to those who are "truly in need"	71
Not individualizing transfers	74
Requiring a consideration in exchange for a guaranteed income	75
Broadening the tax base	76
Starting with a partial allowance	77
Short-term implementation scenario	79
A modest yet individualized, tax-free and cumulative benefit	79
Some revealing figures	80
Progressively relinquishing non-workers from the poverty trap	82
Increasing the net income of the working population	83
Decreasing net income for some and increasing marginal tax rates for others	84
Is a Basic Income politically realistic?	85
The future of a Basic Income and the welfare state	86
Indexing Basic Income to make it more generous	88
Replacing student loan and grant programs and re-evaluating social insurance	89
Strengthening the universal pension plan	92
Making sure that everyone pays his or her fair share	94
The future of social partnership	94
Reconciling justice with democracy	96
Reducing the fiscal sovereignty of governments if necessary	97
Strong social partnership but transparent economic relationships	98
A global Basic Income?	99
Conclusion	101
Appendix A	102
Appendix B	103
Glossary	106
Endnotes	107
Bibliography	123
Index	130

Foreword

Poverty in Canada

For many years, the United Nations Human Development Report has ranked Canada as the best country in the world in which to live. Had the poverty factor — the unequal distribution of wealth in this country — been taken into account, Canada would have dropped to eleventh place. As the gap between the richest and the poorest in our country continues to widen despite strong economic growth in the mid-nineties, future prospects for those living in poverty — the aged, the ill, the unemployed, single parents, aboriginal people and others — remain bleak.

Poverty is not just an unfortunate thing that happens to lazy people. Nor is it the will of God, as some piously claim in quoting that much misunderstood Biblical verse, "The poor you have with you always." Nor is it part and parcel of the human condition. Nor is it just lack of money for some people.

It is also stigma and exclusion from society. It is having to pay more than 50 per cent of your income for rent. It is being told by your bank that you cannot have a mortgage, despite always paying your bills on time, because you are on social assistance. It is being forced to show your health card when you cash your social assistance cheque. Poverty is economic deprivation, but it is frequently also discrimination and humiliation.

Poverty exists for a variety of complex reasons, but not any of them are outside the capacity of human beings to correct or ameliorate. What is lacking is the moral and political will to address the issue realistically and persistently. Instead of a war on poverty, which is hard and requires a long-term commitment, we wage war on the poor, which is easy.

On November 24, 1989, a unanimous resolution of the

House of Commons pledged to erase child poverty by the year 2000. In reality the child poverty rate has climbed since that time. The Honourable Ed Broadbent, who proposed the motion, said, "The motion was not a utopian dream. It was discussed in advance with Liberals and Conservatives, was based on successful precedents in Europe, and had a decade to be implemented. What was required was political commitment."

The concept of a Basic Income

The first time I heard the idea of a Basic Income was in the early 1960s. I knew it as a "guaranteed annual income." I was so excited by the concept that I presented it to a plenary session of Ontario Board members of Children's Aid Societies, but I was laughed out of court. The prevailing sentiment at that meeting was that education would solve our problems of economic disparity, and that the richest, when they understood the disparity, would share their wealth. And they called *me* naïve!

In 1985, I became aware of the MacDonald Commission, with its wide-ranging resolutions on the issue of affluence versus poverty. The concept that government award to every citizen an unconditional, but not necessarily uniform income, has a long history.

This book recognizes that it is time for a fresh appraisal of the concept in our current context. It makes cogent arguments for the potential of a Basic Income and its implementation, with strong critiques from both the Left and the Right. François Blais calls for a rethinking of our social partnership model in a capitalistic society and for maintaining an equitable and just equilibrium between efficiency and equality in our economic relationships.

It is time to look at a proposal for an alternative to the current stagnation of the welfare state and its structural perpetuation of poverty. One of the great strengths of this book is Blais's insistence that economic and moral issues are interdependent and indivisible. Values and ethics are central to the concept. Our economics must not only be viable but must also bring us closer to meeting the fundamental needs of all the members of our society. In the final analysis, justice between people must be given a priority over efficiency.

You may not agree with some of the author's theses, but I guarantee the proposals will stimulate your thinking on this issue. What is important is that the dialogue on the feasibility of implementing a Basic Income for all Canadians is being opened up again by the publication of this immensely readable and knowledgeable book. It will make a significant contribution to breaking the logjam of inaction on poverty and will help Canadians deal more creatively with our national disgrace of poverty in the midst of so much affluence.

Senator Lois M. Wilson
February 17, 2002

Forward to the French Edition

Fifteen years ago, when the term "Basic Income" first appeared, there were no other terms to designate the idea it embodied: an income given unconditionally to all members of a society. Today, the number of names has grown: "Citizen's Income," "Guaranteed Annual Income," "Social Dividend" and so on. And this barely reflects the profusion in the measure's variations and the growing debate it has fuelled.

As we look back on the previous century and look toward the new one, the time has come to settle this debate. It has been stimulated in part by technical research on the redistibutive effects of various ways of funding a basic income at a certain level, for instance, or the effect that different variations of the measure would have on savings, the number of salaried jobs, self-employment, moonlighting or women's participation in the labour market.

It is important to draw some lessons from this research, which falls well short of satisfying our desire for information. But the hottest part of this debate has nothing to do with the product of such research. The systematic, often passionate and sometimes virulent opposition to the idea of a Basic Income from the Left just as much as the Right, rarely stems from a particular empirical hypothesis on its distributive or behavioural consequences, which are often quashed as variations are introduced.

This opposition is more often caused by a mental block over the many paradoxes of a Basic Income. Certainly, it is provided to the rich, but it is done so in the interest of the most disadvantaged. Certainly, it is based on the right to an unconditional income. Its introduction in Canada or Western Europe would no less be akin to establishing a right to work — this no longer being penalized — rather than a right to income — which already exists. And certainly, a Basic Income would necessarily require considerably more money than a guaranteed income that is provided only to the poor, and yet, with respect to what matters economically and what should matter politically, it can end up being less expensive than a conditional system. We cannot end opposition to a Basic Income without clarifying these paradoxes.

Absurdly, opponents often find a Basic Income to be scandalous. By providing an income to everyone, without anything in return, are we not rewarding and therefore encouraging the lazy? Are we not simply using the opportunity to shamelessly exploit workers' productive energy? Even if we could prove beyond a shadow of a doubt that introducing a modest Basic Income would allow the economy to function better and would benefit all strata of society, the moral opposition that it would create, from both the Left and the Right, and for the reasons mentioned above, would be enough to greatly undermine its political viability.

At once an excellent teacher and skilled philosopher, François Blais is in an ideal position, if not to dissipate all opposition to a Basic Income, then at least to eliminate the elements of this opposition that are based on intellectual confusion that impedes understanding or on an insufficient grasp of the ethical arguments that justify introducing the measure in the technological, economic and cultural environment of today. Based on solid information and carefully thought out, François offers an accessible and balanced but passionate introduction to an idea that, after a few fleeting but increasingly persistent appearances, cannot be ignored.

The twenty-first century can do for a Basic Income what the twentieth century did for universal suffrage. If it keeps to its promises, it will be due in large part to the talents and efforts of François Blais.

Philippe Van Parijs
Professor at Louvain Catholic University
and founding member of the
Basic Income European Network

Acknowledgements

Many people were kind enough to pass their comments along to me at various phases of the book's development. I would especially like to thank Marie-Claire Belleau, Jean Bernier, Danielle Blais, Pascal Couillard, Sonia Chabot, Robert Dutil, Jean-Pierre Derriennic, Jean-Yves Duclos, Marcel Filion, Paule Halley, Maurice Lagueux, Robert Nadeau, Yannick Vanderborght and Philippe Van Parijs.

In the spring of 1999, I had the honour of being received as a Fellow by the Hoover Chair of Economic and Social Ethics at Louvain Catholic University. I was warmly received and was fortunate to be surrounded by top researchers. The documentation centre for the Basic Income European Network is located there and I was able to leisurely complete my research in ideal conditions.

To finish, I would like to warmly thank Philippe Van Parijs, who was the first person to introduce me to the principles of a Basic Income. It was the spring of 1993, while we were travelling together from Quebec City to Montreal. True to his generous nature, Philippe took the time to explain, probably for the thousandth time, this unsettling proposal. As usual, he was patient and attentive to my many critical comments. Philippe Van Parijs is certainly one of the greatest intellectuals that I have had the opportunity to meet in my career. I am indebted to him.

Introduction

Discussion about the future of the welfare state has stagnated. Proposals for dismantling it or for draconian cuts to social security have succeeded in conditioning the mindset of a large and influential part of the population. Even the intellectuals, who not so long ago portrayed themselves as the guardians of social democracy, are being swayed by these proposals or are even supporting them with blind enthusiasm. There are many reasons for the success of this neo-conservative brand of thinking. The main one, in my opinion, is that "progressive" thinkers have failed to take note of the successes and also the failures of the welfare state in the West over the past fifty years and to formulate policies that are better adapted to our times.

What I can do to rekindle debate on social justice and the future of the welfare state is rather limited considering the size of the job ahead of us. I was lucky enough, however, to be introduced to the idea of a Basic Income (BI) a number of years ago by one of the most enlightened minds on the topic. With many others (intellectuals, researchers, activists), I became convinced that the idea deserved to be clearly outlined to the general population so that it no longer remained the exclusive domain of a group of social policy experts. A BI should be at the heart of welfare state reform. The goal will not be to dismantle the welfare state but to make it more just and better adapted to certain principles that I will explore in more detail in the second chapter.

The role of introducing what appears to be such a surprising and, in some respects, paradoxical proposal, did not necessarily have to fall to a political philosopher. An economist, a sociologist, a social worker and others could have done it just as well without automatically being characterized as incorrigible utopians, as are philosophers who attempt to work on practical issues. But things did not turn out that way. I ultimately decided to produce this work for a variety of reasons. Debate on a BI did not seem to be getting underway. Certain initiatives had led me to believe that well-intentioned people without a full grasp of the concept would launch it clumsily and improperly. Finally, I felt that I was personally ready to introduce such a proposal. This work reflects, for better or for worse, some of my knowledge as well as my intellectual and social concerns.

Who is this book for?

This book is intended for the largest number of people possible, since the issues involved in a BI affect everyone. The challenge is to find the best way to reach such a wide audience. As an academic, I have mastered a technical discipline as well as the jargon that goes along with it, which I use selectively. I am used to writing for a very select audience made up of other academics who are active in my field and who share this same jargon as well as the same way of presenting and supporting in-depth and, often, dry issues. I do not question this way of doing things. I could have produced an academic work on a BI that would have met the regular academic criteria (furthermore, there are many excellent such works). This approach, however, would have alienated a large segment of the population that I wanted to reach.

For this reason and others, I decided to write a book that does not get bogged down in technical details and that provides an overall view. I also tried to adopt a personal, sometimes emotional, tone rather than an overly academic one in order to motivate readers and, I hope, urge them out of their intellectual apathy. My university colleagues will certainly criticize me at times for making some simplifications. I apologize in advance, hoping that they too will concentrate on the essence of my argument. I may not have been entirely successful in popularizing this work. If this is the case, I accept full responsibility. Perhaps it illustrates the complexity of the issues that I have raised and our unfortunate tendency to simplify everything to the extreme.

What can this book change?

First, this book may help change certain ideas that no longer correspond to our times. This work will disturb those who have trouble thinking outside the box on political issues. In fact, the Left and Right are divided on the topic of a BI, and often for similar reasons. This puts its defenders in a delicate position since they have to learn to argue differently, often in a way that reaches beyond these simplistic political categories.

A history of political ideas teaches us that the fact that some debates last as long as they do cannot always be explained by conflicts of interest between antagonistic groups, or by the profoundly intractable issues involved. On the contrary, within each serious disagreement there could be a significant amount of truth that applies to everyone. This partly explains why political debates often turn into fruitless dialogues that ultimately reinforce each other's convictions rather than generate a true discussion of ideas.

If we did not live in a democracy, the importance of such a situation would be relative. But since this is not the case, our duty as citizens is to find a way to direct the part of truth that we value toward a greater whole, in order to reunite with those who share the same political institutions. Naturally, this means constantly arguing our case and reformulating our initial positions when necessary. We also have to put aside the clichés and slogans that may have ensured our political success, but that have become outdated and are often detrimental to whatever improvements we are seeking. It is also important to look for a consensus that is not exclusively predicated on self-serving support for our position, but which also incorporates the positions of others within a more cohesive political doctrine. Constantly seeking criticism and integration with our adversaries is the only way that we can advance our ideas, whatever they may be. We can only rely on ourselves to achieve this proposal, which is essential for democratic life and social progress.

A BI, therefore, is a demanding proposal that requires a huge effort both morally and intellectually. It proposes daring solutions to neglected yet fundamental problems. It rekindles issues that were believed to be dead. It revitalizes noble ideals from the past that we hurriedly dismissed due to failures in socialist initiatives. Finally, it brings to a new light the requirements for justice and social partnership, and allows all of those who are fighting to achieve them to finally take the offensive, armed with a realistic, yet passionate, alternative.

Naturally, the second thing I would like this book to change for readers is how they perceive poverty and exclusion. These social problems should not be considered as part and parcel of the human condition. In fact, they are primarily caused by inadequate economic and social arrangements in which we have the power to intervene. To change anything, however, we have to agree upon the necessary steps to take and fully grasp the exact nature of the difficulties that we want to overcome. Of course, our world has become very complex. Changes take time to implement and rarely live up to our expectations. Powerful interest groups work to ensure that their prerogatives are maintained and can effectively mobilize public opinion to their advantage, if necessary. Public opinion is demanding, obstinate and sometimes cynical and, whatever else it may be, not easily convinced. This is the world we have to live in. Now, more than ever, we need a clear vision of the problems that urgently have to be addressed. We also need ideals that inspire people to join us and that will help us to fully appreciate every achievement along the way, as small as it may seem. Without these points of reference, we too could be swayed by the fatalism and pessimism of our times. Implementing a BI could be one of the ideals that are noticeably absent today. It is a simple yet radical idea for changing our world and allowing a better life for those who truly need it.

What does this book cover?

In setting out certain important ideas in Chapter 1, I have tried to present a BI as an instrument against poverty and exclusion. This is not the only virtue of a BI, but it is certainly the one the public will respond to the most, since it is shocked by the presence of so much poverty in the midst of prosperity. I have therefore focused on concrete issues that regularly make the headlines.

In Chapter 2, I discuss more theoretical notions such as efficiency and equality. I felt this discussion was necessary for readers to fully understand the diversity as well as the similarities of possible justifications for a BI today. This chapter will also examine the economic and social realities that force us to rethink social partnerships in advanced capitalist societies. Globalization of the economy and work reorganization play an influential role, even though the need for a BI was felt well before these realities had become firmly entrenched.

Chapter 3 is devoted to the important issues of political feasibility and implementation. People are often struck by the "astronomical" costs of a BI. If there are indeed costs, however, they happily have little to do with what traditionally has been claimed. Remember that the goal is not to add a BI to programs that have already done their time. Logically, it has to be implemented by gradually and intelligently substituting it for various social and fiscal policies.

1

Waging War Against Poverty Instead of the Poor

Essential background

Let us start with a simple definition: *a Basic Income is an unconditional income that the government awards to every citizen*. It therefore constitutes a guaranteed income for all: students, workers or non-workers, men or women, rich or poor, young or old — from birth to death. This non-taxable benefit should normally, but not exclusively, be financed through other employment and capital earnings and should replace, either entirely or partially, the main income security mechanisms currently in place: social assistance, family allowance and pensions, various personal and business tax credits, the student loan and grant program, certain social insurance plans, and so on. "Unconditional" does not necessarily mean "uniform," however, and considering the individual needs of children, adults, pensioners and the disabled, the amount of this BI could be adjusted.

That being said, there is no doubt that this constitutes an authentic base income that will allow people to freely make life choices according to what is good for them and their loved ones. In a period of decline of the welfare state where "proactivity" and "the targeting of populations at risk" remain the only solutions that our governments have to offer, a BI revolutionizes the way we approach the battle against poverty and exclusion.

The proposal for an unconditional income for all has a long history.[1] Until recently, however, it was considered a utopian dream for moralists and visionaries who were not overly concerned about proving the measure's feasibility.[2] It was not until the 1960s and 1970s that the idea was taken up again and studied in more depth, particularly by economists wanting to demonstrate that this was not only a realistic proposal, but also one that was more efficient and more just than traditional measures.[3] This certainly lent some credibility to the proposal, which many people felt was still lacking. Today, the BI is receiving considerable support worldwide, particularly from Nobel Laureate economists[4] and top intellectuals.[5] It constitutes an alternative in its own right to the stagnation and uncertainty that has plagued the welfare state over the last few years. Those who claim to care about the future of social democracy can no longer ignore such a reform.

A BI is necessarily disconcerting because of the many disciplines and, above all, the many ideologies of its supporters.[6] Economists emphasize the need to simplify our social assistance programs, which have become tangled webs that are complicated to manage, ineffective in the battle against poverty and, above all, incompatible with the new realities of the labour market. Unionists consider a BI as a means of warding off the negative consequences of the new economy: unemployment, tenuous jobs and stagnant wages for a large segment of the population. Some feminists subscribe to it because they see it as a way of improving the situation of women who are economically dependent, without locking them into the position of spouse or at-home mother. And partisans of a social economy or the "non-market" sector consider it as a means to finance socially useful activities for which private or public funding is lacking or even non-existent. Young people support it because they see it as a better way to finance their studies and as a launching pad into working life. And finally, for social assistance recipients, a BI would simply mean the end of the stigma associated with conditional assistance programs. Its universal feature would allow them to regain their dignity, which has been put bitterly to the test over the last few years by exclusionary workfare* policies and increasingly humiliating control measures.[7]

---

* Derived from the word "welfare," this term is used somewhat pejoratively to designate income support measures that are strictly conditional upon some form of work.

These are only some of the reasons given by an increasing number of people in the world today (intellectuals, politicians, activists, environmentalists, religious figures, financiers and even anarchists) in support of an unconditional income for all. This diversity in points of view is certainly an asset but also a challenge. It is an asset because such an imposing reform proposal requires as much support as possible from the main groups in society. And it is a challenge because it multiplies the risk of confusion and error. A BI cannot solve everything, but it is an important step among many that our society needs to take. Happily, the reasons given above are all valid in their own right. However, we need to incorporate them into a broad and cohesive perspective that takes into consideration what we can justly and realistically accomplish. This is what I will try to do in this work, although I hardly claim to respond to all the questions that inevitably arise from such a significant reform. Others will hopefully bring forth their own ideas to advance the process in their own way. A BI is too important an issue to rely on a single vision of the future.

A Basic Income or Guaranteed Annual Income?

The BI concept is known under a host of different names: Guaranteed Annual Income, Social Dividend, Citizen's Income, Social Wage, Universal Basic Income, and so on. The names themselves have little importance. Their usefulness depends on whether or not they help us to understand the concept. Changing them certainly does not have any impact on the structure of what we are trying to know or explain. Since a BI is already an extraordinary idea, we simply have to do everything we can to choose names that have the least negative connotations in order to better promote the concept to the public at large.

So why choose "Basic Income"? I believe this term is best because it minimizes the risk of misunderstandings or incorrect associations. These will inevitably still occur, and in the case of a BI, selecting a name can be problematic.

A few examples of possible names

To illustrate the problem, let us look at the term "Guaranteed Annual Income." In Canada at least, this is the most widely known term. When I mention BI for the first time to people, most say something like, "Oh! Are you talking about a Guaranteed Annual Income?" This never fails to embarrass me and I admit that I have been tempted to go along with this term just to make it easier to start conversations. This term, however, is probably not ideal. It is true that a BI constitutes a form of guaranteed annual income, but we still have to agree on the meaning of the words. There already exist, in most industrialized countries, social assistance policies that offer guaranteed annual income support to the most disadvantaged citizens. This takes the form of social assistance in Canada, *revenu minimum d'insertion* in France, Aid to Families with Dependent Children in the United States, Income Support in the United Kingdom, *minimex* in Belgium, and so on. These benefits to the most disadvantaged are well known for their conditionality and, unfortunately, the exclusion and dependency they foster. We should not confuse this type of "Guaranteed Annual Income" with the solution offered by a BI, which coincidentally tackles the main weaknesses in these kinds of policies. To be satisfied with this term, we would have to add "unconditional" before "Guaranteed Annual Income." But this formulation seems a little long, and there are other options.

The term "Social Dividend," although not used as much and considered by some to be more outdated, has its good points. First of all, it evokes the moral vision underlying the claims of the first philosophers who argued for an unconditional income: Thomas Paine and Charles Fourier.[8] However, in Canada, this term is too often associated with the Social Credit Party which, in its good years, placed at the heart of its program the astonishing proposal that the central bank would pay a dividend to each family (and not to each citizen). The founder of the movement, British Major Clifford H. Douglas, believed this generalized benefit to be crucial in addressing the inability of bank systems in advanced capitalist regimes to reflect the enormous productivity gains of industrialization in the available money supply.[9] The idea itself wasn't so bad, but its funding raised questions by those who legitimately feared the inflationary pressure of such an expansionary monetary policy. The Social Credit Party had its glory days in Alberta and British Columbia. It eventually evolved into a right-wing political movement with increasingly conservative views. Its founder drifted into oblivion along with his Social Dividend project.

The term "Basic Income" has widely been adopted and preferred to "Basic Grant." It clearly illustrates the important idea that the goal of a Basic Income is not to replace, even partially, all other possible forms of revenue, particularly work revenue, but rather to ensure everyone a security of existence to which it will always be possible and, in many cases, easier, to add additional revenues.

Both "Citizen's Income" and "Universal Basic Income" can create misunderstandings. "Citizen's income" for example clearly underlines the unconditionality of the measure but is marred by a dubious republican connotation. The goal of a BI is certainly not to foster better citizens that are more involved in public affairs or in community work, although neither is it against this. The term "Universal Basic Income" has a connotation of abundance that can work against it. Universality implies we give to the rich as well as the poor, while it is the poor, and not the rich, who will have their situation improved by such a policy. In Canada and elsewhere, therefore, we have to stop speaking about "universal" health insurance, education and old age pension plans, where the main beneficiaries are again the most disadvantaged. If words are conventions, we better cling to those that are already well in use, even it means qualifying them along the way. The term "Basic Income" appears to be commonly used and I have decided to go with this term. This should not prevent anyone from choosing "Citizen's Income" or even "Guaranteed Annual Income," if they prefer those designations. Aristotle said that the word dog does not bite. Yet we still have to find a name for the animal. The main thing is not to get caught up in unproductive wrangling over words, and to quickly initiate meaningful debate that focuses on the key features of the proposal and not on its name.

The unconditionality feature

Some people find the unconditionality of a BI to be both disconcerting and annoying. This is quite understandable. In a way, nothing is ever unconditional, including a BI. To qualify, you have to be a resident or citizen of the country distributing the benefit and this, in turn, depends on sufficient government tax revenues. Some feel that simply adapting the amount of the benefit to a person's age or disability is in itself a violation of the unconditionality principle. I should clarify something here. The "unconditionality" of a BI takes on its full meaning when we compare such a measure to existing social assistance programs, such as the Canadian welfare scheme, managed by each of the provinces. These programs, along with all guaranteed minimum income formulas that I know of in the world, are based on a triple conditionality feature:

- eligibility for benefits and the level of these benefits are strictly subordinate to other disposable income of claimants;
- these benefits take the household composition into consideration and a reduction is imposed on couples and all those who are in a position to share housing costs;
- it is generally understood, and sometimes required, that recipients actively take steps to re-enter the labour market by taking a training course, participating in an internship to keep up their skills, or demonstrating their "goodwill" through community work.

These conditions form the core of our current social assistance programs for the most disadvantaged and justify the use of the somewhat sinister term "last resort assistance." A BI is comparatively "unconditional" in the sense that it allows us to get rid of the three preceding conditions:

- it is granted to everyone without a prior means test (cumulative rule);
- it is paid to individuals rather than households, irrespective of the disposable incomes of other household members, whether they be parents, spouses, lovers, friends or children (individualization rule);
- it does not demand in exchange any requirement to work, to engage in some form of "qualifying" activity, to take any training or to participate in an internship (freedom of choice rule).

The idea is certainly generous, but the immediate response is usually that it is suicidal on the budgetary front and socially irresponsible. How can we give everyone such a benefit, while poverty and exclusion rage on and we cannot even meet our current needs? The answer could well be that unconditionality is exactly what we need, at least as defined above, in order to free ourselves from such phenomena as the poverty and unemployment traps that selective income security programs have created and maintained. Increased conditionality will only result in further poverty and exclusion. Let us explore the reasons why.

Understanding poverty in industrialized nations

In a country as prosperous as Canada, poverty hit 16.9 per cent of the population in 1998. This proportion decreased at times, but as a whole, the number of poor has continued to rise since the 1970s. There were over 5 million poor Canadians in 1998.[10] And there is no indication that such an increase will discontinue — on the contrary. Globalization of the economy, a marked increase in wage disparities and the unemployment rate are not at all reassuring, even though we are currently in a period of relative prosperity that has led to a noticeable decrease in poverty. Canada is not alone in this situation. In fact, over the last number of years, most Western countries have experienced an increase in poverty and, particularly, in wage disparities.[11] In these countries, the 1970s began with a relative stagnation in the battle against such inequalities. The 1980s followed with a perceptible and sustained increase in wage disparities that reduced the appreciable gains made after the Second World War to former levels. The United States, as a worse example, is now in the same situation with respect to wage disparities as it was in during the inter-war period. Canada is faring much better, but still appears to be swept up by the same phenomenon. How can we reverse this trend of increased destitution?

"Non-working" poor

Before we can find a remedy, we have to make the right diagnosis. The image of the poor as disabled, sick, isolated or even mentally challenged no longer corresponds to the new forms of poverty in Western nations. These new forms affect those who are able to work but are not working or who, even when they have a job, are no longer able to escape poverty. How has this happened? Let us start by examining poor households. In Canada, these are more or less divided into two equal groups. The first is made up of non-working poor.* They depend on income support programs to survive, particularly social assistance programs that are financed by federal and provincial contributions. This group consists primarily of individuals who are able to hold a job but who cannot find one, or who face the impossible situation of giving up their status as social assistance recipients.

Their situation has therefore changed dramatically in only a few decades. In fact, when the welfare scheme was being implemented in the mid-1960s, most recipients were considered unemployable. The new policy essentially tried to improve their lot and to simplify eligibility requirements by replacing the range of programs formerly allotted to this clientele, such as old age assistance, assistance for the blind, assistance for mothers in need and assistance for disabled persons.[12] At the time, it was difficult to foresee that scarcely ten years after being implemented, this new scheme would literally be invaded by a new clientele able to work but no longer able to meet their basic needs. In retrospect, this situation no longer seems surprising. The evolution of the economy and structural flaws in our conditional social security programs jointly placed a segment of our population into a situation of dependency, necessarily turning them into non-workers.

"Working" poor

The other group of poor is composed of households that are active† in the labour market but whose incomes remain inade-

---

* Economists use this term to designate people who, as opposed to the working poor, do not have any employment earnings.

† Economists use this term to designate people who participate in the labour market and have salaried jobs.

quate. Let us call them the "working poor." Just like non-workers, their numbers have continued to rise over the last few decades. This is primarily the result of a major restructuring of the labour market, in which a growing number of low-income workers are no longer able to make ends meet. This, in turn, is caused by the increase in part-time and short-term jobs and, particularly, by the relative stagnation of the minimum wage, on which a large number of these low-income workers depend.

In Canada, individuals making the minimum wage must work an average of fifty hours a week to ward off poverty. If they have three dependents in their care, they have to work no less than ninety-four hours a week.[13] The real value of the minimum wage has progressively declined over the last twenty years and this shrinkage in buying power of low-income workers is not just unique to Canada; it is found in most industrialized nations. What would have been unthinkable during the post-war boom has become the hard reality for those with small jobs: the fact that holding a job, even a full-time job, no longer represents any guarantee whatsoever against poverty. The fiscal policies implemented by both levels of government for this category of workers have done nothing, or very little, to stop the groundswell ushering them into poverty.

Fighting against exclusion without increasing poverty

We now know that to combat poverty, we need measures that will resolve the situation of non-workers and workers alike. An immediate response is to require governments to invest more in benefits for the disadvantaged. This is exactly what anti-poverty groups across the Western world have been consistently and ardently demanding for years. Let us look at a dollars-and-cents example of what such an exercise would entail. Statistics Canada estimated that it would cost 16.3 billion dollars to release poor Canadians from poverty in 1995 only.[14] This may seem like an enormous amount, but it basically covers the loss of income preventing the poor at that time, workers and non-workers alike, from reaching the low-income cut-offs established by this federal organization. Things have certainly not improved since then. Benefits awarded to social assistance recipients are generally between 40 per cent and 60 per cent of these cut-offs, according to their household composition and the region they live in. As for the working poor, they rely on their salary plus a few additional benefits such as family allowance or other family tax credits. In some cases, the standard of living of workers verges on that of social assistance recipients.

We can argue about the relevance of the instruments used to measure poverty and their justification but this will not change the fundamental problem I am trying to illustrate. In fact, even if the amounts cited above (or other amounts, according to the poverty measure used) were available, we would not achieve the desired results. The obstacle we need to overcome is structural, and no longer budgetary. It is this obstacle that has made our governments more or less ineffective in the battle against poverty over the last few years. If nothing is done, it could soon render them totally powerless.

Giving more to the jobless?

Let us take a look at the problem. Since the respective situations of workers and non-workers are different, the first reflex is to develop policies specifically for each of these groups. For non-workers, it seems clear that we have to at least increase the assistance level by augmenting the amount of the benefits already being awarded, particularly those distributed by the welfare plan, which are their mainstay. Such benefit increases are regularly demanded by anti-poverty organizations. Unfortunately, this kind of demand puts our governments in a terrible dilemma that has nothing to do with their financial capability.

We do not live in a vacuum. Efforts to redress partially, or even fully, the loss of income of non-workers necessarily have repercussions on workers. The incentive for the poor to keep a job decreases proportionally with the gains made by non-workers. In fact, it is normal for the working poor to measure their relative advantage in working by the income differential separating them from social assistance recipients. By providing supplementary resources to these recipients, we decrease accordingly the advantage in working for low-income wage earners. This means that when a significant increase in social assistance is not accompanied by an equivalent increase in the income of the working poor, we do not end up improving the situation of non-workers, but actually increase their numbers. We therefore need increased financial resources to meet the demand and find ourselves with a new group of non-workers, which is not good for them or for society.

The difficulty we have today is essentially linked to the structure of our assistance mechanisms. Their conditionality restricts any effective redistribution policy toward non-workers. The poverty of this group may well be on the rise, but without the tools to avert this trend, everything we do risks making the situation worse. This explains why some of our leaders and their advisors have adopted a defeatist, sometimes cynical, attitude toward poverty. Their resignation causes them to increasingly focus on the situation of the working poor, under the false assumption that the injustice suffered by them is necessarily more serious in virtue of their effort to keep their jobs. This pro-worker stance stems more from a feeling of powerlessness than from any moral conviction. Unfortunately, it sends a strong message to people with otherwise good intentions that they should support workfare policies and measures that control how non-workers and workers alike allocate their time. I will come back to this later.

Increasing the minimum wage?

But what can we really do for low-wage earners? The most attractive solution would be to try and reshape wages and general working conditions as they were long ago. This could mean, for example, sufficiently indexing the minimum wage and legislating to restrict temporary or part-time work. In the case of the minimum wage, to use the figures cited above, a 25 per cent increase would be needed right away for an individual working forty hours a week, and I do not even dare to think of what kind of increase we would need to allow a family to live decently! Furthermore, this does not take into consideration the short-term and part-time jobs which, in 1976, were clearly less numerous than today. Such increases may seem inaccessible in the short term, but contrary to what we might expect, the gist of the problem is once again structural and poses an obstacle that is even more cumbersome than the one causing the resignation we talked about above.

A quick, and even staggered, increase in the minimum wage that does not take company profits into consideration when distributing salaries would only make most of these jobs non-viable, therefore creating more unemployment with the resulting closures. Our economy would lose a whole category of jobs whose salaries would be unable to meet this new threshold and, for the second time, we would have increased the number of non-workers. We then find ourselves with the following dilemma: do we need to increase salaries, with the real risk of eliminating jobs that have become economically non-viable and increasing the number of unemployed who will then bolster the ranks of social assistance recipients? Unless we move gradually, increases in social assistance or the minimum wage will necessarily kill jobs, causing us to lose on all counts.

Avoiding the situation of favouring one group over the other

Although they do not like to talk about it, the anti-poverty fight has become a true nightmare for our governments. Even if we were to use all economic resources imaginable, we would never come up with a satisfying solution unless we were to disassociate income from work, at least partially. As we try to improve the situation of the most disadvantaged, we have to avoid an alternative that forces us to chose between helping workers or non-workers first. The situation demands that we find a solution that tackles the difficulties of both groups alike. Before presenting what I feel is the best option, I will cover one last constraint. It has greatly contributed to turning our guaranteed minimum income schemes into veritable machines for reproducing poverty and exclusion.

Poverty and unemployment traps

Our contemporaries are not any lazier or any less resourceful than those who came before them. An increasing number of them, however, find themselves completely excluded from economic activity and totally, or significantly, dependent on government benefits. This situation can be explained by many factors stemming from economic conditions and the conditional nature of our social security programs. Neo-conservatives believe our programs are too generous and do not provide a sufficient work incentive for recipients. They are wrong on the first point but perfectly right on the second.

When it is more worthwhile to do nothing than to work

Programs such as social assistance in Canada utterly dissuade their recipients from working, given the 100 per cent tax rate that their work earnings are subjected to. In fact, in these programs where eligibility is always contingent upon a means test, recipients must hand over every dollar of their employment income up to the amount of their benefit. The loss is clearly significant and can even exceed 100 per cent if we add job-related costs (clothing, day care, transportation, loss of certain advantages related to the status of recipient, et cetera). The poorest in our society are therefore those hit by the highest effective marginal tax rates.* How can we then criticize them for not making more of an effort to climb out of their dependency?

Remember that social assistance recipients feel the effects of this excessive penalty even after losing their status as a recipient. Take the case of an individual receiving $500 per month before finding a small job that gives him or her a net income of $750 per month after deductions. For all this effort, including going to work each day, the advantage when compared to social assistance comes out to $250 per month. At first this could still seem attractive, but over time many individuals will ask themselves if it is worth it to leave their status as a recipient in exchange for such modest earnings, especially considering the time and effort demanded by the new job.

Labour economists refer to this tax aberration that locks recipients into an effective tax rate of 100 per cent as a poverty trap, which has many devastating consequences. It inevitably encourages moonlighting, marginalization and even criminal

---

* The marginal tax rate equals the tax rate for all secondary income. For economists, it constitutes a significant variable in measuring an individual's work incentive. The "effective" (or implicit) rate is a way of considering the tax treatment of certain benefits.

activity. Recipients lose all interest in the working world, from which they feel increasingly alienated. They lose the initiative to get to work on time and the desire to do a good job. They sooner or later become stigmatized by employers under the false assumption that the culture of dependency has turned them into unreliable and unmotivated employees. How can workers be motivated when the payoff is so little?[15]

When living with one or more people only makes things worse

There are other effects of the poverty trap that are not as well known but are just as harmful. When using household earnings rather than individual earnings to calculate assistance payments, we end up drawing more people into the trap. Household members become mutually dependent and the efforts of one are automatically eliminated by the dependency of the other. Like their parents, young people are locked into the trap and start believing that they will inevitably follow in their footsteps. Single mothers decide to stay at home with their children rather than taking a job that does not meet their needs. Pregnant adolescents achieve status as independent recipients and gradually fall into dependency and isolation themselves.

The governments' levies on the benefits of those living together discourage mutual aid. Members of a couple who separate receive more individually than they do when they stay together. Young people who share rent see their benefits fused into one. And finally, single women end up with men who flee the scene since they have little interest in helping them with their living expenses or in being investigated by social assistance employees. By non-individualizing benefits, we create many detrimental effects and paradoxically increase the isolation of recipients.

Deconstructing a culture of poverty

Traditional social policies have created a veritable subculture of poverty and exclusion that has been perpetuated from generation to generation.[16] We now have to free the millions of our fellow citizens from the traps that have forced them into a situation of utmost financial and personal instability. This will take time, but there are some concrete measures we can take right away. If we agree on my overall depiction of difficulties so far, then we have to find a solution that can act on three different fronts simultaneously:

- we need to increase the benefits of non-workers without increasing the number of non-workers;
- we need to improve the situation of the working poor without decreasing available jobs;
- we need to decrease the marginal tax rate of the non-working and working poor in order to get rid of the poverty trap.

Another route to take: Basic Income

What can a BI do to solve these difficulties that have been well known to social policy experts for at least thirty years?[17] Let us start with the third point relating to the poverty trap. In a way, what is urgent is not so much making the rich pay more as making the poor pay less. We therefore need to find a way of decreasing their effective marginal tax rate, reducing it from the current level of 100 per cent to a more acceptable rate. Those currently eligible for benefits could then keep a larger part of their employment earnings and increase their net income, while at the same time doing something useful for themselves or for others. Naturally, the difficulty lies in the fact that any improvement in earnings (potential or real) of non-workers necessarily has an impact on the work incentive of the working poor. This phenomenon was mentioned earlier. It clearly encourages workers to reduce their work output to a point where their employment earnings are sufficiently decreased so that they can take advantage of the same arrangements as those of non-workers. We therefore risk a wave of new social assistance applicants. These tax aberrations allowing workers to voluntarily reduce their time at work without any impact on their aggregate income are referred to as the "unemployment trap."

Fighting the unemployment trap while avoiding workfare

To ward against this new trap, we need to further integrate social security with taxation in order to keep workers at their jobs, while encouraging non-workers to free themselves from their dependency. The challenge is enormous: establishing a tax structure that is as harmonious as possible between the two groups to avoid threshold effects that are detrimental to one or other of these groups in their effort to escape poverty. The most radical neo-conservatives propose that in order to achieve such a harmonious marginal tax system, we simply need to abolish all social allowance programs and no longer provide any form of relief to the poor. Workers would therefore see their relative situation "improve" with respect to that of non-workers, who would find themselves on the street but would be "freed" from the unemployment trap. Such a proposal is not, in my view, either realistic or acceptable. In the same vein, other neo-conservatives and conservative politicians have for several years been proposing workfare measures to make the situation of non-workers less appealing, thereby forcing them to return to work. These measures are modern versions of the workhouses found in England in the nineteenth century. Some American states have been experimenting with workforce more or less systematically for some time. Costly and ineffective in terms of re-entry into the labour market, such measures provoke serious injustices by placing into the hands of employers a workforce that is compliant, cheap and deprived of basic rights normally granted to other workers.[18] On this point, teachings in history are valuable, since workhouses were also places for recruiting and exploiting the poor.[19] Now, close to two centuries later, are we prepared to commit these same mistakes and injustices?

Finding a different way of "taxing" the poor

We can do a lot better than instituting workfare or making radical cuts to benefits. To ensure that the tax rate of social assistance recipients is no longer 100 per cent, we have to stop "taxing" their benefits by removing the requirement that benefits be repaid as soon as recipients find work. The resulting tax effect would make the benefits cumulative.

People would justifiably cry foul, saying that social assistance offices would be inundated with applicants. Who would want to pass up on an offer that allows the most disadvantaged to keep every cent of their social assistance income? That is why it would be better to distribute this allowance to everyone right away, irrespective of their financial resources, and recuperate the necessary funding for the BI through tax. In the end, a BI is the easiest way to fully harmonize income security and taxation and, as such, ensure similar marginal tax rates for both the poor and the rich. Workers will obviously enjoy higher incomes than non-workers but the latter will see the poverty trap replaced with a better tax incentive that will reward their efforts and initiatives. By providing an allowance to everyone, poor and rich alike, we can better protect our fellow citizens against uncertainties and situations of dependency with respect to an authoritarian spouse, irresponsible parents, an unfair boss, an overly zealous social assistance employee, and so on. Income security in a world that is constantly changing and is as complicated as ours has become just as crucial as other forms of social partnership. Canada and many other industrialized nations can be commended for a similar achievement in the field of health care, where the young and old, healthy and sick, rich and poor alike share the costs associated with sickness and accident risks.

The public remains committed to the principle of universality in health care. Moreover, it is something we are quite proud of, and those who claim the rich should pay for their own health care because they have the means to do so are few and far between. This is highly understandable: we know that if our tax system is effective it is because the rich pay a huge share. We can do the same thing with income security, which should also represent a guarantee for all. Conditionality should be reserved for taxation, which makes everyone's earnings known, and not for the social safety net.[20]

Improving opportunities for job holders

What can a BI do with respect to our second objective, which is to improve the economic situation of workers without reducing the number of jobs, as would inevitably occur with a pronounced increase in the minimum wage?

As we have seen, since the benefit is universal, non-taxable and therefore fully cumulative, low-income workers will be able to benefit from it as much as non-workers. The BI will therefore increase their net income while maintaining their employment earnings. It is a more intelligent way of improving their revenue than by relying on wage increases that may never come, that may come too late, or that are not based on sufficient economic resources, thereby creating an increase in unemployment. A partial disassociation of income from work for this segment of low-wage earners allows us to achieve anti-poverty social objectives without the counterproductive effects that traditional measures have on the job market. On the contrary, a BI would potentially render jobs viable that are no longer viable right now because they fall under the level of social assistance benefits or the current minimum wage. It would therefore become a tool to support low-income jobs by financing the potential holders of these jobs rather than their bosses. Certainly, since the benefit is paid out unconditionally, no one would be forced to accept the jobs. A guaranteed income would even increase workers' autonomy with respect to their employers, since they could rely on a subsistence income that is separate from their job. But at least these jobs would have the opportunity to exist. We often fault the industries that encompass such low-income jobs for not meeting the demands of the new economy and for being afraid of structuralizing effects on the economy. This may well be, but it does not prevent them from having minimally structuralizing effects on the persons or communities who need them. A secondary income on top of their already disposable income would allow these people to remain active, to improve their know-how and to reintegrate more easily into the more lucrative segment of the job market.

Finding a more distributive structure that is better for non-workers

Where we might fear a BI would fail is in eradicating poverty among non-workers. If we understand that it would now be possible to raise the amount of their benefits (transformed into a BI) without necessarily increasing the number of non-workers (since workers would receive the same benefit), do we not have to acknowledge that this would occur at the expense of the anti-poverty movement? How can we increase support to the poor if our resources are being divided up among everyone and not among the people who need it the most?

To support the argument for a BI, we need to continue to separate income security from taxation. By increasing the amount of the BI and consequently adjusting the tax rates for the population as a whole, we can achieve redistributive objectives that are more substantial than those in place today.[21] First, we will no longer be subjected to factors as conditional as the wage structure, as is now the case, to determine the amounts to be paid out. The only actual constraint we will have lies in our collective wealth and this should increase more easily once we have eliminated certain detrimental employment barriers. We will then have a more substantial allowance, certain low-income but enjoyable or useful jobs and jobs that are much better paid, without having to worry about the deterrent effect that the measure could have on any particular sector of the economy, since it will be fully integrated and all economic agents will be subject to its financing and distribution terms.

Because the BI is given to everyone, it can also do more in the anti-poverty fight, since we are not forcing the least fortunate to provide proof of their misery. The targeting of recipients and the increasing complexity of current programs undermine their effectiveness. Often, those who may be entitled to some form of assistance or other do not take advantage of it, either because they do not know it exists or how to get it or because they find such dependency embarrassing. Remember that poverty is not simply a matter of insufficient income. It also has an effect on self-esteem and the range of options at our disposal. By giving to everyone, we ensure a social safety net that is as wide as possible without having to discriminate between the "good poor" and the "bad poor" and without stigmatizing people as we do today.

* * *

The goal of this first chapter is to outline some general ideas about a BI that I will come back to in the following two chapters. As we have seen, it is not a proposal with a pretext for increased exclusion; on the contrary, it constitutes a means of re-entry into the labour market for hundreds of thousands of our fellow citizens. In my mind, this is one of its greatest virtues. An unconditional income is more effective against poverty in the sense that it helps both non-workers and workers alike, while avoiding the negative effects of traditional income support policies. Our society needs a mechanism such as this to respond to such problems as destitution and exclusion from better-paying jobs. To prove this, however, we need to open our minds and understand the paths that lead individuals and groups with diverse ideologies to support a BI. This measure will only be politically feasible if we can prove that it meets the fundamental needs of members of our society, that it is economically viable and that it brings us closer, more than any other conceivable solution, to social justice.

2

Reconciling Efficiency and Fairness in a Changing World

Two values not to be separated: efficiency and justice

We cannot hope to change our world by preaching virtues that are out of people's reach or ideals that go against their deepest interests. Instead, we need to identify their motivations as well as the institutions that best respond to their interests, and steer them, if possible, toward our ambitious objectives.

Arguments in favour of a Basic Income can generally be divided into two groups. The first focuses on the best way to achieve the socio-economic objectives of the contemporary welfare state. These arguments are made primarily by economists concerned about efficiency, development and job creation. They are important, since a BI has to prove that it is realistic and, in many aspects, superior to traditional forms of social protection. The second group of arguments unites ethical beliefs regarding our social partnership obligations to all citizens, in particular the most disadvantaged.

My goal in this chapter is to illustrate how these two approaches, both economic and moral, are interdependent and reinforce one another. If a BI is achieved one day, it will likely be because it has done a better job of balancing the concerns for socio-economic efficiency and social justice than competing proposals. In the following pages, I will try to show why a BI is the best solution.

*Efficiency and justice do not need to compete
with one another*

Efficiency and justice are both values and not facts. People generally hold these values in esteem because we live in a world where our resources are limited. If the earth's resources were inexhaustible and accessible to everyone, we would no longer have problems concerning economic justice and efficiency, since, theoretically at least, we would not be faced with competing needs or the pressure of using our resources more efficiently. Unfortunately, this is not the world we live in. That is why, in most spheres of human activity, particularly social policy, we have to find an intelligent way of reconciling these two values.

Many people believe that efficiency and justice are necessarily opposed to one another, that distributive justice, for example, can only be realized to the detriment of economic efficiency. This misconception is hard to break. However, social justice theories, both past and present, teach that there are many reasons why justice, particularly economic justice, remains inseparable from practical values such as efficiency.[1] I will explore two of these.

First, irrespective of what our principles of justice may be, we need to determine the most efficient ways of achieving them. Justice is not utopian; it wouldn't serve much of a purpose if it could only provide our citizens with dreams and illusions. Of course, any concept of justice must set out certain ideal standards, but these have to remain accessible to people and their institutions in order to fulfill their key role and to promote progress rather than the status quo. Since justice is a fundamental social value, we have to be as conscientious as possible when formulating its principles and determining the means to achieve it or bring ourselves closer to it.

The second reason why any thoughts about justice should automatically include efficiency comes from a metaphor that is unfortunately all too familiar: sharing pieces of the same pie. I should emphasize that our tendency to represent economic justice as some form of pie, in other words, as something that is permanent, divisible and separable, greatly undermines our understanding of the issues surrounding distributive justice. If justice were to be compared to sharing a pie, we would probably, in the name of equality, have to slice it in identical portions. Unfortunately, this is a false comparison. What we commonly refer to as "collective wealth" is the product of numerous economic elements, most of which have none of the attributes mentioned above.

A nation's wealth is the dynamic and evolving result of the combined actions of millions of individuals who unknowingly maintain, or have maintained, economic ties that benefit some more than others. These individuals act within a framework of rules, expectations and incentives that guide their production, exchanges, consumption and savings. They feel a certain entitlement to the fruits of their labour and are mindful of the constraints, including the way in which socio-economic institutions distribute what they have freely acquired. In fact, any redistributive arrangement can have the effect of increasing or restricting the potential wealth to be shared. If the taxes are heavy and constraining, for example, and they effectively reduce the incentive to produce, save and invest, the global value of what can possibly be shared will simply be less. We therefore have to consider the potential economic effects of any principle of justice. We also have to ensure that it corresponds to political and economic arrangements that do not undermine personal initiative and effort but that, on the contrary, allow us to channel some of this initiative and effort toward cooperation and social partnership.

Attempting to define these two values

What exactly do we mean by efficiency and justice? We could be tempted to define the first as the "best possible use of limited resources." Unfortunately, this definition is inadequate since the term "best" is ambiguous and could be understood as it relates to justice, which is not primarily what we want. According to economists, the term "best" has a much more precise and more neutral meaning: an arrangement (commerce, production, distribution) is efficient or optimal if, and only if, it is impossible to increase one of the terms without decreasing any of the others. They generally find a "Pareto-optimal" approach more rational, in reference to the great Italian economist from the nineteenth century, who was the first to formally define the modern concept of economic efficiency.[2]

I should point out that this criterion of economic efficiency, which currently pervades trade journals and even our daily discussions, is totally immune to fairness. In fact, for any initial distribution, it is sufficient that the value of only one of its elements be improved and that no other be lowered, irrespective of the relative situation of the other elements. This criterion therefore has a purely aggregate function, stressing the global value of what is achieved as a whole over the relative position of the individual elements. This certainly does not hold true for justice, particularly distributive justice, where we generally expect that the advantages of one group be reduced to benefit another.

This important distinction between the aggregate function and the distributive function leads us to a first conclusion with respect to the relationship between efficiency and justice. If we were always faced with pure distribution situations, in other words, arrangements where an improvement in the options of one would result in at least an equivalent reduction of the options of the other, we would then constantly be arbitrating between efficiency and fairness, and the relationship between the two would effectively be antagonistic. Happily, this is not always the case. This explains why a better distribution is not always achieved at the expense of growth and can, on the contrary, be positive for growth, as we will see later on.[3]

Economists have a definition for efficiency, but philosophers, true to their image and to our times, have not been able to agree on the meaning of justice. Certainly, they have proposed various criteria, but none of these seems to have brought about any consensus. The most sceptical (or the most cynical) may conclude that it is an arbitrary matter of taste and preference that is impossible to resolve. Yet the definition for justice cannot be reduced to a matter of taste. One's tastes apply only to oneself, and to ask someone to justify them is neither useful nor relevant. The principles that guide the nation's policies, on the other hand, concern everyone and can have enormous repercussions on people's lives. The "preference" for women to be treated the same as men, the "preference" for abolishing undue privileges of certain groups and the "preference" for implementing a BI one day need to be debated and justified, as do all great moral and political issues. It would be really irresponsible of us to allow these important values to be dependent upon popular tastes, emphatic appeals to tradition or the power of influence of those who feel they could benefit the most from having them realized.

The goal of a modern democratic state is normally to achieve the ideals of freedom and equality of which we are all, in varying degrees, heirs and beneficiaries. We can do this first of all by recognizing for each person a certain number of freedoms that provide the legal and political framework for exercising individual privileges. In traditionally democratic societies today, these so-called "formal" freedoms are easily recognized, although it is still necessary to debate their specific scope, the potential conflicts between them and the best way of implementing them in social and political organizations. By simply granting individual freedoms, as important as they are, we are not ensuring freedom and equality among citizens since their value, that which they allow us to tangibly achieve, differs considerably from one person to another according to their living conditions. You have to be completely blind or fanatical to believe that a person who is poor, sick and uneducated could be just as "free" as his or her rich, healthy and educated neighbour, even though they have the same rights. We therefore expect economic justice to specify the principles that will allow us to restrict certain socio-economic advantages in favour of a greater equality in living conditions. Such equality is yet to be defined.[4]

"Everyone according to their worth" is not an acceptable standard

Most of us feel that inequalities that are beyond our control should be corrected or compensated in some way. In a culture that defends equality, we cannot tolerate leaving people to their sorry fate simply because they were less fortunate at birth than others. This is a good starting point for us to build on. The difficulty is in determining where our responsibility for others begins and where it ends. This difficulty, in turn, stems from how we reconcile freedom and equality. Too much freedom can be detrimental to equality, while blind appeals for equality can diminish freedom, as testified by the disastrous experiences of communism in the twentieth century. There seems to be a fine balance between the two. Because we value freedom, we feel that the choices people make should bind them. At the same time, we recognize that these choices are born of circumstances that individuals do not necessarily control and that they are carried out in an environment where there are a great many inequalities.

None of us were able to choose the place and time of our birth, the family we grew up in or the options that our family were able, or not, to provide. We know, however, how important these and other such factors are in determining the type of lives we lead.

Some feel that they deserve their enviable situation and try desperately to justify it by evoking their modest social origins or the efforts and personal sacrifices they have made to get where they are. Nevertheless, the predispositions that affect personal effort, perseverance and sacrifice are not equal either. This also holds true for other characteristics that shape our personality, such as a sense of initiative and risk-taking, curiosity, empathy, and so on. Our education, surroundings and simply our personality will inevitably foster some of these qualities and hinder others. Even though we are all entitled to find happiness, it is clear that our prospects vary enormously and that we have to continually fight against our relative weaknesses and disadvantages in order to fully enjoy the advantages we do have, whether they be few or many.

The factors of inequality permeating our lives do not stop there, since individual differences are exacerbated by our heavy reliance on other people. In fact, the value of each of our advantages depends in large part on other people lacking such advantages, on the social demand for these advantages and on the level of economic and technological development that we work in. Salaries provide a good overview of the situation. The same effort and output lead to a wage that is totally different depending on the place, time or economic situation within which the work is being carried out. If goalie Patrick Roy had been born earlier, he no doubt would have been a teammate of Maurice Richard, but his income would be nothing at all like what he earns today, in an environment where the salaries of professional athletes are primarily based on astronomical television broadcasting rights. People therefore cannot seriously claim that they totally deserve the fruits of their labour, since the demand for this labour is socialized and dependent on conditional factors that none of us can claim to control or deserve on our own. Division of labour, for example, is based on productivity gains. Unfortunately, this leads to greater income disparities, to the extent where, for reasons of efficiency and professional freedom of choice, we put up with wages that are determined in large part by supply and demand. In the best of circumstances, this situation could result in an effective allotment of salaries, jobs and services, but it is no less arbitrary in terms of fairness and justice and nothing compels us to accept it. On the contrary, we need to judge society by the way in which it limits the effects of the many inequalities that permeate our lives.

What kind of equality are we looking for?

If we cannot discriminate between what belongs to us and what was brought to us through our circumstances in life, then what can we do to create a more just society? Do we have to try and share everything equally? This is neither feasible nor recommended. First, in order to achieve total equality in material conditions, we would have to continually intervene in everyone's private lives so that we could distribute the earnings and profits that individuals may well have realized under freely authorized conditions of exchange. This strict interpretation of equality would necessarily violate the most fundamental freedoms and can only be conceived in extremely authoritarian and collectivist societies.[5] The fact that we were born with certain talents and into certain surroundings should never preclude us from using these advantages toward personal or collective achievement. At any rate, such an interpretation is not ideal in fighting against the inequalities of life circumstances. In reality, if we are sensitive to the situation of those who have inherited fewer advantages than others, we should no less accept the existence of economic inequalities, particularly if the profits they generate are spread out among other members of society.[6] To facilitate a BI, we need to implement a flexible and permanent wealth distribution mechanism that would benefit a larger number of people, while at the same time preserving everyone's self-esteem and increasing the opportunities for personal growth. What then should be the criterion for fairness? What level of BI will bring us closer to a just distribution? I will try to answer these and other related questions at the end of this chapter. For now, let us start by examining how a BI can do more for us than current social policies. To do this, we will first take a look at the impact of these policies on the economy.

The economic role of social policies

Most economists agree that, to run smoothly, a modern economy needs government intervention to mitigate weaknesses or failures in market mechanisms. Competition and private initiatives can be excellent for effectively, or almost effectively, distributing consumer goods such as food or computers; however they do not optimally meet all of our needs. In principle, there is no single economic arrangement that would have all the required virtues, especially considering the diversity of our needs and the many ways of responding to them.

In its economic interventions, the government plays two big roles: (i) it can foster a better distribution of wealth and opportunity among members of society (this is referred to as pure redistribution); and (ii) it can increase the levels of production, consumption and savings (this is known as efficient redistribution). Naturally, these roles can be carried out simultaneously. In this and the two following sections, I will underline the modern government's role of efficient redistribution that we have a tendency to neglect today.[7] I understand that the welfare state is faced with a host of criticisms right now, but we need to keep in mind certain central economic ideas before dismissing it out of hand.

Limits of market mechanisms

Economic theory teaches that, in a market of perfect competition, goods and services should be optimally or efficiently allocated. This does not mean that the distribution of these goods would conform to "justice" or "fairness" (remember that the Pareto criterion is independent of any particular form of distribution), but these goods would at least be available in sufficient quantities and at the best prices possible for those with the means to pay for them. For such a perfectly competitive market to exist, we need to unite many conditions, some of which, depending on the type of economic goods required, are unrealistic on a practical level. As well as a total absence of any form of monopoly, a perfect market would require: (i) that consumers and producers have complete information (with respect to both the present and future); (ii) that no good can be consumed for free and that no indirect cost can be imposed on anyone during the production or consumption of a good; (iii) that market agents are indifferent to one another and driven exclusively by their quest for personal economic gain; (iv) that prices be transparent and stable and that no transaction cost be attached to the exchange of goods or services. Unfortunately for free market supporters everywhere, in most practical situations these conditions will never be brought together. In circumstances where efficiency can be achieved by simply reverting to the dynamic of competition, most economists agree that government intervention can be useful and sometimes even necessary. Up to what point? This is difficult to answer with any precision. The problems in question are empirical in nature and answers will always be controversial and tied to specific market conditions. We should realize that while non-intervention does not always ensure efficiency, it cannot be said that interventionism does any better. Nevertheless, the history of industrialized economies in the twentieth century has shown that a market economy can benefit significantly from many forms of government supervision and support.

For the past twenty years, government intervention in economic and social life has received a lot of criticism. It is our job to ensure that these criticisms, stemming from widely divergent points of view, are put to public debate, while avoiding passionate outbursts as much as possible. One of the mistakes made by the Left is to transform any discussion on the future of the modern welfare state into ideological quarrels and fundamental choices of society. Such an attitude uselessly polarizes the positions. There are certainly questions regarding the aims of social policies that deserve more discussion on the political stage.

A large part of our disputes with respect to social and economic policies, however, results from analyzing the means and not the ends, and this is naturally where a factual analysis becomes important. Those who defend social democracy in the name of justice have to avoid reverting foolishly to the equation that a greater government presence in economic activity necessarily favours justice. The experience of organized economies in former communist regimes has shown that this is not the case. Similarly, evoking slogans such as "access to health care is a right" does not demonstrate that attaining this right requires government involvement. Eating is certainly a right that is just as important, yet we generally feel that the market can take care of allocating the necessary goods.

What the government can do to help the economy

To counter market deficiencies, the contemporary welfare state uses three types of measures: regulation, public production of goods and services and direct (explicit) or fiscal (implicit) benefits. I will cover these quickly by focusing on the third category, which concerns a BI.

The first type of support that the government can provide the economy is to establish a stable legal framework that fosters civilized dealings between people and the resolution of conflicts through an impartial arbitrator. Laws protect economic players, their entitlements, dealings and documents of title, thereby helping the market to run smoothly by emphasizing the foreseeable aspect of our actions. The government can also legislate to counter monopolies, guarantee the value of currency, ensure the quality of goods and services, prohibit civilian gun licenses, and so on. The necessity for this type of intervention is well known. I will therefore move on directly to the second category.

Certain kinds of goods and services cannot be provided by private enterprise. National defence and the police are two classic examples. Other goods and services can be provided privately but are better off being nationalized or heavily supported through legislation because producing them privately would be expensive or not efficient. This is especially true for education and health care.

In industrialized societies, education generally benefits from strong government intervention. There are many good reasons for this that have nothing to do with the economy. We cannot underestimate the importance in a society such as ours of having a qualified and sufficient workforce. We can only achieve this by implementing a public education system that is largely financed and regulated by the government, one that is capable of joining together all strands of the population, not just the elite, as we have seen in the past.

Accessible health care for all is also vital to a prosperous economy, since illness results in considerable costs to individuals and can greatly undermine their productivity and mobility.

For these two sectors, education and health care, economists generally admit that a free market would not be as effective, for two main reasons: (i) it is too difficult for people to access information on these services in order to make the best possible choices and their bargaining power is often too weak or unfairly distributed; (ii) potential abuses or mistakes by the producers of such services can have overly heavy, even irreversible, consequences. These reasons combined weaken the customary advantages of supply and demand mechanisms for these services.[8] In sectors that are so crucial to the well-being of individuals and society, it seems better to have the government involved. The degree of its involvement, however, needs to be defined after a thorough examination of past experiences and current institutions and practices. Theories to resolve these empirical issues can only provide us with limited help if we do not support them by comparing, experimenting and meticulously evaluating the facts.

The place for income security in a healthy economy

Let us move on to cash benefits associated with the third form of government economic intervention, that which directly concerns redistribution measures such as a BI. If the market were capable of efficiently allocating certain goods and services, this does not mean that employment and capital earnings would be divided satisfactorily, let alone equitably. Remember that the efficiency requirement is immune to resource distribution and is only sensitive to an increase in the total amount. That is why, in a purely capitalist society, extreme wealth could very well accommodate poverty that is just as extreme. It is also why a significant part of gross domestic product in most industrialized nations today is earmarked for individual and family benefits. Such benefits can take many forms: family allowance, income security benefits, social insurance, retirement pensions, various tax expenditures, and so on. These cash benefits naturally have a purely redistributive role, but we cannot ignore the economic gains that result.

The first economic advantage to benefits is that they provide financial security to the population as a whole. This security requirement does not stem soley from pure redistribution. In fact, the quest for security is a central element of the human condition, which also has economic consequences. In competitive market societies such as ours, for example, economic growth and competition can be increased by the degree of security that prevails. Contrary to what is traditionally believed, the economic success of capitalist societies does not rely solely on their success in promoting people's selfish and materialistic needs. Their success results largely from a relative stability that breeds economic cooperation.[9] Capitalism requires investment and commerce to be carried out under strict conditions of security and foreseeability. Increased financial security leads economic players to take certain risks and initiatives, while amortizing the costs associated with potential failures. In the working world, giving benefits to individuals makes it more acceptable to implement certain changes (reorganizing production, introducing new technologies, adapting required skills, and so on) and helps to alleviate the issues arising from the sometimes-costly negotiations between workers and employers. Cash benefits also indirectly reduce the risks and costs related to excessive criminal activity and marginal behaviour, which, in turn, stem from workforce exclusion.

The second advantage of benefits to individuals is that they maintain the demand for goods and services throughout periods of recession or economic slowdown. Since the propensity to save is stronger among the rich than it is among the poor, a controlled redistribution of wealth will stimulate consumer spending. Architects of the contemporary welfare state, Keynes and Beveridge, claimed that to avoid recessions as devastating as that of the 1930s, we needed to ensure sufficient and continuous benefits to stimulate consumption and, consequently, production and economic activity as a whole. Only the government, as an organization with a monopoly of legitimate power over all components of society, appears to have the means to coordinate such a boost to consumption.

Finally, benefits help to maintain the demand for jobs and encourage input during periods of recession or economic restructuring. This is important since, as we all know, full employment is never ensured in capitalist societies, which are always in need of restructuring in order to deal with the many changes in demand or new production technologies. Social assistance measures or direct benefits to individuals are consequently needed to help the unemployed get through breaks in employment and ease their transition to new jobs or training. Workers, as opposed to technological stock, cannot be discarded when they are no longer profitable or needed. We therefore need to ensure their well-being as well as their ultimate re-entry into economic activity and community life.

Challenging the welfare state

When the welfare state is criticized, as it often is today, tax transfers are frequently mentioned. They are criticized for their deterrent effects on: the demand for jobs (since many recipients experience no economic advantage by leaving their current idle situation; the demand for training (since programs rarely ease the transition from worker to student); savings (since in order to be eligible for last resort assistance programs, individuals need to have exhausted some of their wealth). They are also criticized for creating undue tax pressure on government budgets, which have locked us into spiralling debt from which we are only now starting to emerge. Advocates of a BI, particularly those who are most concerned about maintaining economic efficiency, stand behind the first of these two criticisms. As for the debt crisis, it can only be resolved by providing a healthy management of public funds and initiating more dynamic economic prospects, which could favour the introduction of an unconditional income. Before seeing how this can be achieved, let us try to better understand what may have led to the decline of the welfare state and the loss of confidence in it over the last few years. Let us also try to understand why we are compelled to find solutions that are more appropriate for this day and age.

New constraints of a changing world

The modern welfare state took off at the end of the Second World War. In Canada, the social safety net was strongly influenced by the Beveridge Plan, named after the famous British reformer and economist. Beveridge tabled a series of motions in British Parliament in 1942 to prevent England from lapsing into a recession as it had, along with other industrialized countries, between the two great wars. The Beveridge report recommended a strengthening of social security measures through compulsory insurance plans, the introduction of family allowance to compensate for the inability of wages to cover the costs of child support, a universal health care system and the implementation of an integrated social safety net for the most "exceptional" cases. Typically Keynesian, this reform plan responded to the objectives of both effective redistribution and pure redistribution.

The first steps made by the contemporary welfare state

In Canada, Beveridge's ideas were taken up by his student and a professor at McGill University, Leonard Marsh. He was asked by the federal government to develop a post-war reconstruction plan based on the work of his intellectual leader. Marsh, who was assisted by many colleagues and intellectuals, submitted his report in 1943.

The core of Beveridge's and Marsh's proposals was to implement social insurance programs to protect workers' earnings during periods of unemployment and following their retirement. These insurance programs were to be financed through mandatory contributions of workers and their employers. Beveridge and Marsh both concluded that former private insurance systems proved to be inadequate during the Great Depression and that it had become necessary for the government to legislate to compel employers and workers to systematically contribute to a single fund. Private social insurance funds at the time had furthermore been unable to meet the legitimate security needs of workers.[10]

The success of this compulsory social insurance system relied on two basic factors: (i) a high employment rate (in his report, Beveridge foresaw a normal unemployment rate of 2 per cent); (ii) adequate average salaries (the report estimated that one salary should be able to support the needs of a household with two adults and one child). With such an economic outlook, it was estimated that adequate social insurance programs, supplemented by universal family allowance, would allow us to free the population from the grips of poverty.

Income security was limited to a residual role. Beveridge did not like the conditional structure of income security, already anticipating its detrimental effects on work incentive. At any rate, he believed that few people would find themselves being supported by these programs (if we naturally exclude those unable to work, for whom the work incentive problem is not as crucial).

This model of the welfare state proved to be successful everywhere it was implemented. It allowed the Western world to quickly come out of its stupor following the end of the Second World War. During the following decades, industrialized countries attained unparalleled prosperity, a considerable reduction in income disparities and unprecedented improvement in the standard of living of their workers. It was the post-war boom. However, this was not to last.

The end of this model

Starting in the early 1970s, the first failures of the welfare state were being felt. The oil and energy crisis shook the industrialized world with its intensity and duration. This first upheaval was accompanied by an inflationary trend that continued into the 1990s and that is generally blamed on an overly rapid expansion of government expenditures.[11] Then there came widespread unemployment, along with job insecurity and increased wage disparities. Better-adapted redistributive and tax measures protected certain countries, including Canada and France, from too high an increase in after-tax wage disparities. However the two pillars on which the Beveridge plan was built — full employment and higher salaries — now belonged to another time, while the "official" unemployment rate often exceeded the 10 per cent bar in most industrialized nations and one income alone could no longer meet the needs of most households.

What happened? Many things, but we need to focus our attention on three significant trends: (i) an increase in the number of women in the workforce; (ii) the opening of markets and the resulting global division of work; (iii) considerable productivity gains from new technologies, leading to massive job losses in most industries where machines have become economically more profitable than workers.[12] Such productivity gains are not historically uncommon; we experienced similar trends earlier in the twentieth century. It appears that this productivity growth is no longer accompanied by an expansion in production or consumption, as it was in the post-war boom. The service sector that we relied on to revitalize our economy following the decline of the industrial sector now appears to be the first victim of new communications technologies.

Obviously, none of these three structural changes has been bad in itself: (i) the participation of women in the workforce is one of the greatest feats of the twentieth century; (ii) the opening of markets has encouraged capital movement that is indispensable to the development of less-industrialized nations, resulting in economic cooperation, which often leads to political cooperation between peoples; (iii) the introduction of new production technology contributes to increased productivity and an overall improvement in the standard of living. These benefits, however, still need to be felt more equally across the population, which is decreasingly the case.

Victims of the "new economy"

There are thousands of people who lose as a result of these economic changes. Market openness is an example. Since salaries are determined more by the value of work in international markets than in local markets, the winners are those who have the skills that are most in demand and who have the option of working in strategic economic sectors or those that are particularly well unionized. The people who lose the most are obviously those with relatively few skills who are working in sectors that have become weakened by direct competition from similar jobs in other parts of the world where wages are substantially lower. These workers have seen their companies shut down or have had to accept major concessions in their working conditions to try and hold on to their jobs a little longer.

Within this context of heavy competition, the level of required skills plays a crucial role. Those who, for all sorts of reasons, are less prepared (workers with few skills, young people with no experience, powerless families, and so on) simply have no possibility of reaping the benefits of the new international markets. They quickly find themselves with no short- or long-term prospects, and pep talks do nothing to improve their situation. The social insurance mechanisms that once guaranteed our success no longer help those who are excluded from the workforce, since they no longer have even the minimum requirements to be eligible. We find them increasingly caught in the social insurance poverty trap. In a matter of only a few decades, millions of people have become totally dependent on government resources for their survival, and there is no indication that this will change. On the contrary, globalization of trade threatens to produce many more victims from among the least-educated and most-fragile segments of the population.[13]

To find solutions to the above problems, our governments began firing in all directions. A finger was pointed at the welfare state, and some neo-conservative economists believed they would be able to sign its death warrant. Free market and competition came back into fashion and the same governments that just yesterday were standard-bearers of economic regulation felt compelled to present their role as a partner or catalyst in development. Many measures were experimented with: the sale of large public corporations, deregulation, a reduction in social contributions to make businesses more competitive, a reduction in social assistance benefits to encourage people back to work, further opening of the market, development of new technologies to increase productivity, and so on. Despite, or perhaps because of, these actions, unemployment and particularly poverty endure. Furthermore, those who yesterday set their sights on a possible economic recovery, acknowledge today that this makes a mockery of creating well-paid jobs. What was unthinkable in the time of Keynes and Beveridge is now part of our daily lives. These new realities explain how urgent it is to find solutions that are better adapted to our times so that we can successfully reunite economic efficiency and justice.

Economic grounds for a Basic Income

Today renowned economists, financiers from prestigious organizations and even people from the business world support the principle of an unconditional income.[14] For some, this support attests to the seriousness of the proposal. For others, however, this makes it both suspect and dangerous. This uneasiness is particularly widespread among the traditional

Left, which sometimes considers itself the exclusive defender of social progress. Let us remind those who share such fears that striving for efficiency is not itself incompatible with justice, and that the economic justification for a measure is not equivalent to a defence of economic liberalism, let alone the status quo. That is why both the Left and Right must be willing to study a BI in light of its potential economic benefits, as I intend to do in these pages.[15] Strictly prescriptive justifications will come in the next section, which closes this chapter on efficiency and justice.[16]

Ease of administration and transparency of transfers

Relatively simple and coherent to begin with, our social assistance programs have become expensive to manage and complicated to administer. Agencies have multiplied and each new program has its own administrators, who are not always aware of other programs. This type of complexity breeds inefficiency, reduces the mobility of recipients and leads to inevitable waiting periods for citizens who are increasingly lost in the tangled web that has become our social security net. Civil servants no longer have a comprehensive view of things. They have piecemeal information, for example, on the combined effect of tax policies and social assistance policies. This situation can lead to many detrimental effects, such as excessive effective marginal tax rates for categories of the population who normally should not have to pay as much tax on their income.[17] Naturally, conditionality and targeting cost more to administer since we have to pay for the necessary personnel to ensure all of the controls.

In comparison, universal programs will always be simpler and much more transparent. These days, administrators can easily set up periodic bank deposits for those eligible by plugging some information into a computer file. Considerable savings in program management can therefore be reinvested into improving the benefits themselves. Do we not have to acknowledge, however, that all these administrative savings will automatically be cancelled as a result of the enormous waste in benefits to those who do not need them? It was precisely this kind of argument that led to the progressive dismantling in Canada of social assistance programs, such as family allowance. These arguments, however, do not take into account the "income-effect" of any redistributive policy. Let us now try to get a better understanding of what this means.

The goal of a BI is not to improve the net income of the richest but to increase the prospects for the poorest by providing everyone with better financial security. When instituting such a measure, we need to adjust the tax rates to ensure the desired distributive effect on net incomes. This is what we do to finance other universal or public programs such as health care, education, public safety, road maintenance, waterways protection, support for municipal libraries, and so on. With such a tax adjustment in place, we will understand that providing a universal measure to a community does not necessarily cost more since, universality or not, it is always those with the greatest financial capacity who assume proportionally the costs of government expenditures.[18]

The major flaw in the current tax system is that it is not sufficiently integrated with our social assistance plans. This creates various aberrations. For example, in some situations the employment earnings of the most disadvantaged are taxed more than those of the affluent. In addition, people are often unsure of the amount they can rely on, considering the vast array of both direct and indirect benefits to individuals. Our governments award conditional family allowances at the level of family income and at the same time continue to provide tax deductions that benefit wealthier families. Similarly, the amounts allocated for Old Age Security have stagnated for several years, yet the same governments provide the wealthiest members of society with generous tax exemptions to invest in private pension plans. These exemptions, which amount to billions of dollars, constitute huge tax gifts that we all know benefit the well off much more than people with modest incomes. With respect to benefits and taxation, we too often ignore, or claim to ignore, that what we do with one hand can be undone with the other. In the end, a BI would have the advantage of making the amount that everyone receives more transparent. It would also spell out society's obligations with respect to children, parents, young people, the handicapped and pensioners. This kind of transparency is seriously lacking in our current tax system, which inevitably increases the risk of abuse and administrative errors and leads to a democratic deficit for the majority of us who would like to have a better understanding of our rights and ensure that they are respected.

Less bureaucracy and more financial security

Conditional income security programs are constantly being changed in order to better reflect the needs of recipients. One reform follows another and civil servants who administer them have a hard time keeping up with them, let alone understanding their logic. It is well known that administrative complexity and erratic changes breed inefficiency and considerable wastes of time. The infinite increase in the number of recipient categories only makes things worse. Bureaucracy discourages potential recipients, who are tired of the countless administrative headaches, who are embarrassed to be claimants or who are simply misinformed with respect to their eligibility for certain programs.

Protecting incomes while maintaining recipients' preference for mobility and personal initiative is one of the goals of any economically efficient social assistance program, as we saw in the section entitled "The economic role of social policies" in this chapter. Over the last few years, the only remedy that our governments have found to combat the apathy of some recipients is to revert to coercion or forced activity, but this strategy does not succeed simply because it relies on a simplistic and bureaucratic view of human activity.

The administrative complexity of conditional benefits ultimately undermines recipients' mobility. Some recipients adapt their behaviour to program requirements rather than to their own needs. They end up being scared to take risks and avoid situations where they could suddenly lose certain assets, as minimal as they may be. Recipients thereby become progressively more entrenched in their administrative status and can no longer clearly see the benefit of returning to work. This kind of attitude is understandable given the economic, social and even psychological instability that characterizes this segment of the population. Therefore, we have to avoid fuelling their insecurity or lack of understanding about the social assistance system if we want them to free themselves from their dependency.[19]

How did we get to this point? The current complexity of our social assistance programs did not occur overnight; it took years of reforms to weave such a tangled web. Individually, these reforms were not always so bad. Most of the time, they were designed to respond to changes in market conditions and client groups. This is likely where our governments took the wrong turn. Hypotheses relating to market conditions or client groups are often erroneous or out of date and unduly penalize individuals by locking them into categories that do not correspond to, or no longer correspond to, their situation or goals. Of course, we can always make an extra effort to correct our mistakes and add new clauses to our programs. In this constantly evolving world, however, it is probably better to make our social policies as unconditional as possible, resulting in fewer expectations, frustrations and inefficiencies. By doing so, we also allow individuals to adapt their behaviour to rules that are simple, unchanging and known by all.

In traditional societies, the welfare scheme was much less complicated since the few benefits in existence were distributed to stable households. These were made up of individuals locked into social roles with more predictable needs. In modern societies where there is increased marital mobility and where everyone expects their personal life choices to be respected, our expectations about the status of couples, students, pensioners and even children often miss the mark, causing wrongs that could have been avoided.

A BI redresses the uncertainty of conditional programs by offering coverage that gives everyone the same protection for life, irrespective of their choices, mistakes or successes. It certainly does not put an end to the uncertainties in life, but alleviates some of these in the same way that health care has eased the fears about getting sick and not being able to afford treatment. The failures of socialism taught us that it was presumptuous to plan complex economic exchanges between large populations. Similarly, we have to avoid anticipating or defining the matrimonial, family or individual lifestyles and behaviours people will adopt to provide for their most fundamental needs.[20]

Where everyone has the same advantages in working

The conditional structure of current income security programs has negative effects on employment. Generally, it penalizes recipients who work for pay. The type of work these recipients do is, therefore, destined to disappear, to be carried out on the side or to be exported into countries where salaries and social security are inferior. We are more or less resigned to this situation and see it as the price to pay for ensuring that those excluded from the labour market have a minimum standard of living.

This dilemma between social protection and jobs is not insurmountable. We have to maintain a gap between activity and inactivity in order to make the majority of paid jobs attractive. This gap does not currently exist for social assistance recipients, who are taxed at 100 per cent of their earnings, and for the working poor it exists but is too small. I have focused a great deal on the negative effects of the poverty and unemployment traps in the previous chapter, so I will not go into any more detail here except to reiterate their negative impact on work incentive. Let us just say that it is time to re-equalize the tax burden in favour of the have-nots.

There is no reason why benefits to individuals must depend on them not holding jobs, particularly low-paying jobs that are generally more accessible to less-qualified people. We need to ensure work is truly profitable for all and not only those who hold the most strategic jobs in the economy. A BI is a non-taxable benefit, which means that it can be drawn concurrently with varying income levels without any penalty. This fact makes a BI very different from current social security programs, which discourage recipients from holding the jobs that are most readily available. Generally, the surest way for people to get a good job is to have previously held a job that was less ideal but allowed them to develop certain aptitudes, expertise or skills. These jobs are simply not available today to many social assistance recipients and an increase in social assistance would only make the situation worse.

Social democrats today do not have to choose between more social protection, more unemployment and less poverty (as in Europe) or less protection, less unemployment and more poverty (as in the United States). There remains the plausible alternative of a BI.

Supporting poorly paid activities

In a free market, some activities may be paid at an insufficient level for workers to live decently. Traditionally this has been the case for household work and childcare. For a long time, women at home have paid the price for society's inability to recognize the economic and social importance of their contribution. Today, there are countless numbers of these underfinanced activities: business internships, support and assistance to persons in need, return to studies, artistic creation, social economy, handicrafts, business start-ups, research and development, membership in associations that promote quality of life, organic and traditional local farming, and so on. We need people, not recordings, to answer the phone when we want information. We also need them to serve as museum guides, to help the elderly take the subway, to look after children after school — in short to take care of others. "Quaternary-sector" activities are in full expansion, but we have not yet succeeded in financing them appropriately.[21]

We need to understand that "salvation" for millions of unemployed is still possible outside the niches of the new economy. In fact, there is great potential in lesser-paid activities. The low unemployment rate in the Unites States can be explained by a significant expansion of low-paid jobs, particularly those in the service sector.[22] This growth was encouraged by a minimum social protection policy and the success of work income supplement programs such as the Earned Income Tax Credit, a measure which increases the gross income of low-income families and which encourages them to keep their jobs. The ideal situation would be to have an unemployment rate comparable to that of the Americans, but with more security and fewer inequalities.

Our governments already massively subsidize jobs in the public, parapublic, private and community sectors. A BI would allow us to continue these efforts much more transparently and would minimize the risk of patronage and favoritism of one sector over another. In fact, a BI can economically be considered as an indirect employment subsidy (paid out to individuals as opposed to businesses), as is partly the case with health care and public education. We are therefore right in comparing it to a "base income," the goal of which is not to finance idleness but rather to make it easier for people to access many different activities that vary both in content and execution.[23]

More flexibility in work organization

A BI, together with coherent employment policies, could have the effect of revitalizing economic sectors that need it. We now import massive quantities of goods from countries where salaries are considerably lower than ours. This situation creates competition that is impossible to support and leads to the loss of entire segments of our economy.[24] Market openness and technological innovation have different consequences depending on the job sector, although it is generally the less-qualified employees who bear the burden since their jobs can be more easily exported abroad or carried out by machines and computers.[25] Even a modest decoupling of work and income should encourage people to pursue more voluntary activities and make human work more competitive with certain technologies.[26] Such a disconnection between work and income would create a better balance between people's legitimate need for financial security and the flexibility needed in modern work organization.[27]

We have entered a phase of accelerated trade and technological change that requires businesses and their employees to adapt a great deal. Jobs that we used to consider non-standard have become the norm. Some workers are delighted with this new situation while others feel that they are paying the price. With all these changes in the new economy, the best thing we can do is to ensure that material security is based a little less on the job market (as it has been for a long time for many of us) and a little more on explicit forms of social partnership.

Naturally, the activities financed indirectly by a BI are not necessarily those with the most economic weight. However, the main thing is to encourage a greater union of different types of activities, jobs and salaries to satisfy the new economic requirements, while giving better protection to those having the most difficulty in dealing with these changes.

What will happen to the minimum wage?

By encouraging direct benefits to individuals, are we undermining our right to a minimum wage? This prospect is unsettling for those who feel that employers have a moral obligation to pay their workers equitably. The idea of a "just" and "decent" wage has been very important in the history of the social movement and is recognized by certain international conventions.[28]

I question the economic plausibility and ethical value of a minimum wage. I will come back to this in the next section, but let us start by talking about the future of the minimum wage in the context of a guaranteed income.

Are we allowed to eradicate close to fifty years of the welfare state and social legislation and institute a BI in their place? Many radical partisans of an unconditional income, from both the Right and Left, have been tempted by this slightly simplistic idea.[29] Technically, it is true that a guaranteed income already constitutes a salary minimum that is superior in some aspects to wage legislation. First, everyone is entitled to it, workers and non-workers alike. Furthermore, the current minimum wage shares a serious flaw with social assistance: it compromises potential economic activities that cannot be paid at this level. A BI, on the other hand, is never in direct competition with a paid activity (since it is cumulative) and can even make some of these activities economically viable.

So, starting tomorrow should we abandon all work legislation and let the free market define working conditions? I think this would be dangerous. A BI cannot be a substitute for certain major labour laws such as those protecting workplace safety and ethics, those that institute mandatory leaves, that protect contracts or that ease unionization. As for the evolution of the minimum wage, any discussions will remain theoretical, at least until we are able to ensure a guaranteed income that is comparable. The principle of a BI does not require the trading of one security for another. As I said in Chapter 1, as a weapon against poverty the minimum wage has continually declined over the last few years. It would be rash to make any sort of pronouncement on its future and probably irresponsible to rely on a single wage policy for our future financial security. An undifferentiated increase in wages seems unrealistic when the goal should be a return to full employment within an economic context that is very different from that of the post-war boom.[30]

And what about other salaries?

Others fear that an unconditional income would automatically be recuperated by employers anxious to reduce wages.[31] This fear has no basis as long as the benefit remains unconditional and employers have no control over it. Employers, like their employees, will remain entirely subject to the traditional constraints of salary negotiations and will not be able to decide how to allocate money that they do not have in their own hands, any more than they can today. It never enters our minds, for example, that the public funding of health care can unilaterally have the effect of decreasing wages to the benefit of businesses. On the contrary, if a BI can change anything at all in wage negotiations, these changes should normally benefit those in the weakest bargaining position, who are compelled to accept tiresome, unstable or even degrading jobs that no one wants today. These people would no longer have to sell themselves out.[32]

Those who worry about benefits being recuperated by employers should take a critical look at conditional social assistance programs, particularly those with a work requirement. Not only do these employers end up with a rare and coveted resource (work), but they also enjoy the "privilege" of being able to grant recipients an increase in their benefit. With respect to their bosses, these people find themselves in an even weaker position, if imaginable, than that of the lowest-wage earner.

Since a BI favours redistribution to people rather than businesses, it makes workers less vulnerable to the whims of unscrupulous business owners. Of course, as I have continued to argue in this book, sometimes people should have the option of accepting lower salaries. But what is important, for efficiency and fairness combined, is to protect (and improve) the disposable incomes of people most affected by these changes.

Diversifying incomes rather than focusing completely on work

We know that high average salaries encourage businesses to develop production technologies that allow them to replace expensive labour with machines. These productive forces historically help fuel collective wealth but also lead to considerable unemployment in our industrialized societies. Should we worry, then, that a low-wage policy could lead to the emergence of less-productive businesses, which would be detrimental in the long term to community development? No. I do not think that this should be a concern.

Of course, a wise economic policy should not be designed to promote low wages exclusively. It should, however, allow for more differentiated salaries and work systems to coexist. A BI can foster this differentiation in three different but complementary ways: (i) through a voluntary reduction in the number of hours worked (a BI can be conceived as a flexible way of encouraging job sharing); (ii) by encouraging initiative in market and non-market sectors (financed through a benefit provided directly to all citizens); (iii) through the emergence of low-paying jobs, sometimes with salaries that are below subsistence costs for a single person. In each of these cases, the main issue is the same: ensuring that disposable household incomes rely a little less on employment earnings and a little more on direct benefits. Even a minor shift in the work/income relationship will necessarily benefit citizens who will be able to handle the expectations of the labour market more easily without bearing the costs. All we need to do is make sure that the most productive sectors are tapped in such a way as to finance potential workers in the other sectors. A BI would therefore allow us to redefine the traditional objective of full employment by adapting it to the new economic order.

Naturally, all these economic benefits associated with an unconditional income are only conceivable if this income is supported by a coherent and complementary economic policy. We can easily imagine, however, that there would be a negative impact on general productivity and training if too many people choose to carry out less productive activities at the same time or, quite simply, decide to relax and enjoy themselves. Although this is a plausible problem, it will take time before the amount of a BI is high enough to encourage the most-qualified workers to leave their jobs or for students to stop taking work-related courses. In principle, a BI should always ensure that people have an advantage in working or developing their skills. However, we cannot deny the possibility that the value of this advantage will decrease as the benefit increases. This is not a reason to turn away from a BI, just a reminder of plain economic evidence. Similarly, if the tapping of collective wealth demanded by a BI constrained the budget to a point where an economic slowdown were to ensue, we would then know we had reached the highest conceivable level for a given economic period. It is at this stage that we would likely find ourselves arbitrating between efficiency and justice.

A Basic Income and social justice

They may well be inseparable values, but in any conflict, justice should always reign over efficiency, even economic efficiency. After all, the latter comes secondary to achieving a just society, in other words, a society that fosters the peaceful and equitable coexistence of its members. Therefore, arguments based strictly on socio-economic efficiency will not be considered sufficient when it comes to justifying a social measure such a BI. Moral and ethical objections have to be taken just as seriously as practical objections concerning feasibility or utility.

Putting a Basic Income in an intellectual and political context

The crisis affecting the welfare state does not stem exclusively from budgetary and administrative difficulties. A vast intellectual crisis is having a profound effect on its rational and ethical foundations.[33] Our moral beliefs on the subject seem to be increasingly confused, contradictory and sometimes even totally without thought. It is no longer rare, for example, to hear well-intentioned people praise social partnership mechanisms of the past like family and small community. They have forgotten to what degree these mechanisms were discriminatory, inefficient and inequitable. Some become entrenched in their zealous criticism of contemporary liberalism and are incapable of acknowledging the progress we have made in our time. This unyielding attitude has always seemed dangerous to me.

We need to rekindle the debate on the values that should be guiding our social institutions. Unfortunately, it is difficult to rely solely on politicians to lead such substantive debates since they are driven by election-minded logic, focusing on slogans. We would expect that intellectuals, with much fewer speech restrictions, would do a better job, but they are no longer as inspired by social justice as they once were. Let us hope that they will one day climb out of their stupor.

Achieving a BI would require us to regulate on different problems: What scope should it have? What kind of role should it play with respect to other existing or potential forms of social partnership? How should it be financed in the short and long terms? There is no consensus on these questions, which lends credence to the fact that BI supporters belong to diverse ideological families. Of course, I have no intention of resolving these questions in the next few pages. Again, my only goal is to provide an idea of the appropriate ethical grounds for changing how we conceive social partnership, a change that is needed today more than ever.[34]

Giving to everyone, including the "lazy"?

The objection that plagues BI supporters the most is its profound unconditionality. We often hear, even in the name of justice, that we should never distribute benefits without anything in exchange. This objection does not come from malicious, self-centred or conservative people. In fact, I have been able to test this many times. This is a belief that is shared, as much on the Left as on the Right, by people who claim to have a high sense of justice but who feel that this measure requires at least some form of reciprocity.[35] According to this view, everyone has to make a contribution to society, no matter how small. Those who do not, should not be entitled to public funds. Why should there be any form of social obligation to people who are "lazy," "profiteering" and who "voluntarily" put themselves in a situation of dependency?

This concept of justice roughly corresponds to the old idea of corrective justice, where what we receive is always proportional to what we give. Aristotle was one of the first supporters of this idea, which is still more or less widely held today. It also figured prominently in the United States' recent social security reform and it is clear that it plays a pivotal role in the ethical grounds for workfare.[36] Despite this, I find it inapplicable, incoherent and, above all, profoundly unjust.

First, the reciprocity requirement poses practical difficulties, since we need to determine what we mean by "contribution." The many possible points of view on this question should quickly tell us that finding an answer is impossible. Has a woman who has sacrificed her energy and career to take care of her children contributed more or less to society than someone who has worked to build the success of his or her company? Should the artist pursuing his or her creative endeavours be punished because he or she is not contributing enough to economic development? Should we favour instead the well-paid qualified employee working in a factory that pollutes the environment? What about the neighbourhood grocer? Does he or she have any less value than the manager of a large food chain with better prices? And finally, what about someone who prefers to concentrate on the "good things in life"? Does he or she deserve to be judged by ambitious career professionals who leave many victims in their wake? If we think about it, we have to admit that evaluating someone's "social contribution" will always be problematic and biased. It inevitably compels us to consider personal values that are too controversial. In a pluralistic society, a consensus on these values governing the lives of individuals will likely be impossible to achieve.[37]

Reciprocity then poses another fundamental problem with respect to the framework for analyzing justice. Our sense of justice should normally be much less sensitive to lifestyles than to objective circumstances that undermine equality. "Lazy people" are found in all strata of society, which is indeed proof that this has nothing, or very little, to do with our opportunities for success. If society were made up of perfectly equal individuals with the same opportunities for success, we might then expect equal contributions in terms of effort or production. In fact, we have seen in the previous sections that this initial equality does not exist and that, on the contrary, people are forever affected by immense inequalities that they did not choose, but that have a profound effect on their lives. By rewarding people according to what they have to offer, we would necessarily be replicating these inequalities.[38]

We should not be completely opposed to the reciprocity requirement, but we have to make sure that we interpret it correctly. For example, it is clear that laws should be the same for everyone and that there is a general obligation to respect them, irrespective of our social situation, skin colour, sex or political allegiance. This type of reciprocity is an excellent thing in society. It reinforces the feeling of equality between citizens and encourages them to behave as equals.

Inequality of opportunities and circumstances

Is there not the risk that those who decide to take more leisure time rather than working will be exploiting the work of others?[39] Not if they are receiving their due, in other words, what they are entitled to as a full member of society. Social partnership constitutes this particular form of mutual responsibility that binds citizens of the same state. It clearly distinguishes itself from other forms of cohesion that could exist within a family, group of friends or private association. First, social partnership relies on a desire that everyone be treated equally, despite their differences. We have to rely on this principle of equal respect when examining socio-economic inequalities, and not on our concept of what constitutes a valuable or exemplary way of life for everyone.[40]

I always try to teach my students that we cannot define our mutual responsibilities from a moral standpoint, since this creates aberrations such as the one whereby "lazy people" are treated differently according to their wealth. (While the rich have unrestricted access to the wealth they obtained in fortunate circumstances, the poor have to earn their right to a benefit.) Within private relationships, of course, people can demonstrate their personal preferences and deepest-held beliefs. They can, for example, pass on certain values to their children even if the majority of others do not share these values. They are also free to join a religious community and leave when they become disenchanted with its practices. The opposite is true in the political sphere, which is not an association of voluntary members (no one chooses their fellow citizens.) And yet the laws and institutions that govern society remain the same, irrespective of our personal values, religion or origins.[41] This is a good thing. Among other things, it avoids continuous conflicts between groups sharing the same territory. And it above all prevents the most advantaged in society from "choosing each other" and practising an exclusive form of social partnership, which is happening much more frequently in societies where there are considerable economic inequalities.

Throughout our lives, we all enjoy circumstances that are more or less favourable. These can take the form of "internal" assets acquired at birth and then developed through education: talents, personality traits, health profile, and so on. They can also take the form of various "external" assets: family, economic and social backgrounds, placement within the generations, inheritances, chance encounters, gifts, and opportunities of all kinds. Unfortunately, all of these internal or external assets are distributed unequally, either through the luck of nature or through legal or socio-economic arrangements that quickly accentuate the imbalance. Yet these inequalities form the basis on which we live. Some receive a lot; others receive a little. And what about the least fortunate? They are left with illness, disability, the inevitable accident, family idleness and so on. Fate is doubly blind; it largely differentiates in its distribution, while ignoring individual needs.[42]

Ideally, to be equal, everyone in life would receive the same number of these internal and external assets. This would maximize individual growth opportunities. In many cases, equal sharing is impossible since many of the unearned assets are neither divisible nor separable. For example, the unique circumstances that allowed Bill Gates to develop a company like Microsoft occur rarely in life and can certainly not be shared equally. This holds true for scientific discoveries, trade initiatives and gains that are made through sheer luck. We must not let this practical yet inescapable obstacle force us into adopting too quickly the principle whereby everyone is entitled to everything they produce or earn. Allowing producers to have an exclusive right to the fruits of their labour is morally reprehensible since the production conditions themselves inevitably occur in an environment where circumstances are unequal.[43]

The current wealth of our societies is based to a large degree on the combined work of past generations. This wealth includes accumulated capital, scientific and technological knowledge, natural resources, efficient social and economic institutions and so on. As is the case for individual gifts, no one can claim to have a larger right to this collective resource that ultimately defines individual and collective productive capacity. This heritage has to be shared equally to prevent us from reverting to inequality as the basis for organizing the production of goods and services.[44]

Without a recurring distribution mechanism, the market economy and property combined will reinforce initial inequalities with respect to access to capital and all other rare resources, both internal and external. This *ex ante* form of redistribution can be done through a single allotment, as envisioned over two centuries ago by the philosopher and politician Thomas Paine.[45] It can also be realized by distributing a periodic annuity throughout life, a solution that I favour in order to maximize long-term opportunities for the neediest in society.

From this perspective, a just society needs to diminish the effects of the many initial injustices that people face in life. We can do this, for example, by offering free health care or education (education is still, despite what people say, a formidable tool for social promotion and it should be free at all levels.) We also need to ensure that institutions are adapted to the needs of those who are disabled, either physically or mentally, or that we provide them with sufficient monetary compensation. Of course, all of this is being done to a certain degree today. Of all the possible and necessary arrangements, however, we need an unconditional income for each citizen. We can now see that such compensation would not be based on any principle of charity, but on a fundamental right: an equal sharing of the value of all these internal and external assets that life has to offer including, of course, the immense heritage passed down to us by our predecessors. However, we need to ensure that this compensation is unconditional since all eligibility conditions that could be demanded in exchange (training, work, forced activity of any kind) would necessarily challenge the inequality of circumstances that this measure is compensating for.[46]

Redistributing wealth while respecting dignity

The arguments we have raised so far and which we often find in pro-BI literature justify a large-scale and continuous redistribution of wealth, but is a BI the only answer? What about targeted benefits that are subject to a means test? Could they ensure a just compensation as outlined above? These could be part of the solution if justice could be reduced to an economic matter of loss of income. Justice, however, is more importantly about respect, human dignity and each citizen's ability to assert his or her rights.

Selective programs are generally stigmatizing and humiliating for the people that are eligible. They are forced into the situation of petitioners who must show proof of their poverty and put up with constant investigations into their personal life. To be eligible, they are required to have used up a portion of their personal wealth, which increases their dependency even further.

Another problem with targeting social policies is that it divides society into two distinct camps: debtors and contributors. This fuels the idea, particularly in difficult economic periods, that the one group lives at the hands of the other. Recipients often have a finger pointed at them and are subject to the moods of public opinion. The power relationship works completely against them when they make claims to improve their situation. Of all societal groups, they have the weakest influence and least ability to assert their rights. Policies such as workfare do nothing to help them. On the contrary, these policies force them to take jobs they do not want and to work in conditions that are inferior to those of other workers, which firmly entrenches them in their status as second-class citizens.

If justice needs to promote autonomy, dignity and the ability of individuals to assert their rights and be recognized throughout society, then there is a strong presumption in favour of a universal rather than a selective program. First, we would no longer be forcing certain citizens into the situation of petitioners. Second, assistance would be provided preventively in order to avoid the irreversible effects of economic decline.

The unconditionality of a BI makes this measure a true right in the strongest sense of the term: a protection against uncertainty and abuse.[47] Because it is given on an individual basis and without requiring anything in exchange, a BI reinforces the power of those who have much too little of it: people who are dependent on the government, civil servants, spouses or third parties. The basis for its unconditionality is human dignity, which propels us to implement universal rather than targeted programs.

The priority of the right to income over the right to work

The idea that justice is a matter of dignity is clear. In response, do we really have to provide everyone with an unconditional income? Many people still doubt we do and, with human dignity in mind, prefer that priority be given to the "right to work" over the "right to an income."[48] In their view, work provides advantages that are often forgotten about by BI supporters. It promotes individual accomplishment. It stimulates a sense of responsibility, initiative and cooperation. And, finally, it encourages integration into the community. They feel that social assistance programs, no matter how generous they are, can never be as successful, particularly with a program that is as individualistic as a BI, which only further isolates the have-nots, especially if they are completely disassociated from the productive sphere. A BI would therefore be devoted to a two-tiered society made up of a minority of highly skilled and profitable workers and a mass of people who have become economically unproductive but who we need to help for humanitarian reasons. We are told that to prevent such a nightmare, we need to ensure that income security is subsidiary to work and that it does not become a way of life, which is the risk of a BI for a considerable part of the population.[49]

These comments lead me to the following clarification: by supporting a BI, we are not at all proclaiming the end of the "salaried society." I have always been uncomfortable with this common means of "justifying" an unconditional income. Full employment is not necessarily a thing of the past. Furthermore, and for excellent reasons, it is still a worthy objective that I fully endorse. Nevertheless, the workplace has experienced, and will continue to experience, large-scale transformations that require changes to our strategy in fighting against unemployment. We need to find a better way of reconciling income security and the flexibility of work organization. For the reasons mentioned above, a BI could be part of an overall strategy in this respect. I will not come back to this point, except to renounce as many times as necessary the connection that people are trying to make between a BI and a catastrophic effect on work.

Let us now get back to the issue regarding the right to work. If we insist on viewing this as a right, then it is true that we should always favour the right to an income over the right to work. In fact, the right to work relies on a legally vacuous principle (it has not been used in any society). The reasons are simple: paid work is a socialized activity that is dependent, both in its definition and its salary, on the demand of others. I may want to become a carpenter or a voice teacher, but I will not succeed unless others pay me enough for my services. My right to a particular job is therefore tied to the right of others to choose their own job as well as the goods and services that they want to buy. No form of social organization is able to meet such competing desires.[50] A totalitarian regime that centrally determines needs and demands could naturally come close to the objective of providing everyone with a job, but at this point, we transform the right to work into an obligation to work. We should not distort this principle of the right to work, particularly when other solutions allow us to come close to it, if not to the letter then at least in spirit.[51]

As for the integrative advantages of working, should we not at least recognize that a job is fundamental to self-esteem and therefore a BI could never succeed as well in this area? Should we not recognize that a BI could end up creating a society populated by the scarred victims of economic globalization? I am not sure of the merits of either of these statements. Jobs as we know them today — that is, jobs that are salaried and involve a significant division of duties — are a relatively recent invention. We should therefore try not to assign any inherent virtues to them. In fact, many people view their jobs as a practical necessity.[52] This does not make them bad workers and it certainly does not make them bad citizens; they simply have more gratifying tasks to carry out in their free time.

In fact, the symbolic value that we attach to work depends a lot on what others are voluntarily prepared to sacrifice in terms of spending their time on someone else's product. If this were not the case, any recognition associated with work would, for the most part, become meaningless.

Jobs have always been a source of integration for some and a source of exclusion for others. The financial and symbolic advantages in having a job vary greatly, as do the interest factor, the degree of difficulty, the future prospects it may bring and its social recognition. At any rate, job benefits are distributed unequally since, in a market economy, the job is a rare resource, subject to intense competition. Well-paid, socially valued jobs are necessarily harder to find than others. Because of this competition, jobs are allocated unfairly, and those at the losing end feel dissatisfied with their situation and their status in society. Our tendency to emphasize the merits or necessity of a job is particularly odious for those who are dissatisfied with their occupation but who see no alternative.

Paid work is also the source of profound inequities. Compensation is based on many factors that are morally arbitrary but that allow a segment of the population to appropriate a considerable portion of collective wealth, which, we remember, is based on the work of previous generations and not exclusively on individual output. The wage and price system may have many virtues, but it will never ensure a just distribution as long as it refuses to take people's needs into consideration. The market essentially follows the logic of competition and innovation, and we can only expect it to perform tasks that are compatible with its impersonal function of producing and allocating resources. That is why we have always needed to replace these redistributive flaws in the market with social assistance mechanisms that respect the explicit rules of social partnership.

By tolerating the fact that wage earning is the best route to income, we implicitly support the unequal benefit that results. The division of work in the world today increasingly allows those who have inherited the most rare and coveted assets to benefit more since they now have the world as a potential client. In contrast to all those who reap huge profits from the way work is organized today, from the increased mobility of both capital and people and from new technologies, there remain those who, with factors of production that are less in demand, find themselves without work or locked into a job for which they have no real interest or recognition. The first injustice would not be as bad if the second did not exist. Those who profit the most from the work organization and its exchanges therefore have the responsibility of dealing with unemployment and poverty since, visibly, the new economy does not benefit everyone equally.[53]

By providing an unconditional income to everyone, we do not put an end to the inequalities created by salaried work, but we reduce their most harmful consequences. In particular, we help prevent workers who have factors of production that are the least in demand from losing their dignity by selling their labour power at any price to survive. Work can take on all its value as a liberating or an integrating activity once it is no longer entirely defined by the marketplace.[54] That is why, in all logic, the "right to work" must be understood as the "right not to work" and as an opportunity to engage in activities that are not exclusively subject to the standard rules of the marketplace, of supply and demand.[55] Presented this way, a BI opens up a new coherent perspective with respect to the "right to work" and puts into place the resources to carry it out.[56]

Increasing opportunities for those who have the least

People often ask me to specify the ideal level of a BI that would come closest to meeting the requirements for a just compensation that I have outlined so far. Should we be satisfied with the current level of social assistance for a single person? Should we not instead be trying to approach the poverty indexes, such as recognized low-income cut-offs? Should we even attempt to go beyond such levels? Before answering this question, I need to make a few clarifications. Remember that, despite appearances, a BI is fairly flexible and can be used for generous as well as modest redistributions. That is one of the reasons, albeit not the most decisive one, why it is supported today by distinct ideological groups who have different priorities with respect to economic distribution. In choosing a criterion for distributing social wealth, we therefore separate the minimalist approach of simply maintaining the disadvantaged segments of society from a more generous approach that I feel closer to.

The criterion for wealth distribution that I prefer comes from the principle of justice whereby we have to always try to find economic and institutional arrangements that improve the situation of the most disadvantaged in society.[57] It is because of this principle of justice that I became a supporter of a BI: I feel that the winners of such a reform would be those who suffer the most from current economic changes. That said, this criterion has to be specified so that we can better determine its content and scope. I acknowledge that some of the problems that I will cover in this section will appear to be technical and even a little abstract, but it is sometimes good to remind ourselves of the complexity of the issues at hand if we want to make distributive justice a priority.

Let us start with a first constraint that affects the way the government organizes and finances its other responsibilities toward its fellow citizens. We have seen in the previous sections how the contemporary government has been pursuing various fundamental missions. The rationale for social assistance can stem from a quest for efficiency as well as social justice. The issue at hand is to determine what part of a BI will take the form of public services and what part will be distributed monetarily. Generally, BI advocates assume that cash benefits are better than those in kind, simply because they provide more freedom of choice. We can reverse such an assumption, however, after examining the advantages (economies of scale, fairness, stability, better long-term protection, and so on) of certain government services offered exclusively to those with the lowest incomes. Many critics of the modern welfare state criticize it for having developed erratically by submitting itself to the pressures and interests of the most influential lobby groups. This is partly true. The welfare state must never be seen as sacred, but as a tool that we should not be afraid to use to measure efficiency of performance and social justice. Distinguishing between what is essential and what is non-essential, particularly when a more generous redistribution of benefits is at stake, is well worth the effort.

The second constraint is of a completely different kind. Justice is naturally a matter of financial resources but also of freedoms. It would be unacceptable, even with the goal of higher production and redistribution, to transform a segment of the population into slaves (for example, the most talented who we generally expect to generate great wealth). These two economic spheres (production and redistribution) have to respect such fundamental freedoms as the right to choose a career and the right to privately own personal assets. Although no one today is opposed to these ideas, they are still worth thinking about.

I mentioned above that strict egalitarianism was not conceivable for caring societies. We cannot use the same approach to ensure equality as we do to ensure that we have trimmed a hedge properly: cutting off the ends! Societies group together individuals with legitimate and diverse aspirations. Their individuality makes certain socio-economic inequalities inevitable, and even desirable, since it is normal for effort and initiative to be rewarded. Therefore, the problem is not the existence of socio-economic inequalities but their enormity and the fact that they bear no comparison to what is socially, and above all, morally acceptable. If we believe in freedom, then we should lose no time in addressing these kinds of inequalities, while keeping in mind that certain inequalities are not harmful and can actually be beneficial by instilling a sense of initiative and motivation that collectivism tends to discourage. Therefore, strict egalitarianism is not a valid choice for a BI. Furthermore, if we were really committed to the idea, we would have to impose a tax rate of no less than 100 per cent on collective earnings from all sources. This would lead to a clearly suboptimal redistributive solution. Between a society that is perfectly egalitarian but poor and a society where inequalities are tolerated but where the most disadvantaged are freer and better treated, I believe we should choose the second option.

These remarks lead me to a third constraint that I will call the constraint of economic sustainability, which stems from the fact that wealth redistribution is necessarily dependent on the conditions of its production. Both have to be continuous and stable to avoid problems such as creating uncertainty for those who are most dependent on benefits. As a result, any distribution criterion has to be flexible enough to adapt to economic requirements as elementary as work incentive, investments and savings. As such, we have to put into place institutions that are well suited to an efficient production and allocation of goods and services and which promote capital accumulation and productivity. If we do not worry about such elementary economic conditions, we could end up with a dangerous form of voluntarism where the most indigent pay the price. The redistribution dynamic cannot be blind to the requirements of a healthy economy and should stimulate it whenever possible.

The constraint of economic sustainability also has repercussions in searching for a just distribution criterion. It precludes us from setting thresholds that do not take our economic potential into account. A good part of the discourse on redistributive justice, however, is based on the claim for a "minimal threshold for all," which could well take the form of a poverty line or coverage of fundamental needs. This popular conception of justice is not bad in itself and we may want to submit a BI to this kind of criterion. As we saw in the previous chapter, a BI is better suited than competing formulas to fighting against the new forms of poverty, which explains why most anti-poverty groups are interested in it. The issue is knowing whether the anti-poverty fight, in as much as poverty is identified by a minimum threshold of resources for all, best represents our obligations.

My first comment is this: in my opinion it is impossible to agree on what poverty is. The threshold that would allow us to define it may well be too low or too high with respect to our economic capacity. In the first case, we would justifiably wonder why the threshold was so low. In the second case, we would have to ask ourselves if it is truly responsible to establish objectives that, once achieved, could have counterproductive consequences for even those we want to help. These two reasons justify in my mind why we have to avoid using static criteria, such as the poverty threshold, in favour of more dynamic criteria that can evolve with indicators of wealth or inequality.

One of the criticisms that has to be made of the contemporary welfare state is that it has not sufficiently managed to ensure reciprocity between the rich and the poor in trying to reduce the extent of economic inequalities. It is true that we are not used to hearing such dynamic criteria in public debate, but it is never too late. Poverty lines should remain as they are: indicators that allow us to track changes in poverty. They should in no way preclude us from doing a more in-depth analysis on what everyone is owed.

I will now get to the last constraint that I feel is important to address. Economic development is not everything. We also need to think about sustainable environmental protection. Wealth needs to be produced and redistributed in a way that respects the needs of future generations. We need to institute the necessary resources that will encourage future generations to treat the most disadvantaged in their society the way we should be treating ours. It would be wrong to set a high BI level for the current generation if we ended up with a level of production that caused serious environmental deterioration. The care we provide to the neediest in our society today must not undermine the next generation's ability to do the same. Environmental sustainability necessarily restricts economic sustainability and requires that all compensation mechanisms be aligned with sustainable development. I do not think that this requirement will lead to many objections in principle, but I wanted to bring it up here since it means that we will gradually have to implement some form of environmental accountability that will allow us to maintain productive capacity for future generations.[58]

Now that we have been reminded of the four constraints of redistribution, let us return to the main topic of how we should distribute the wealth. I have argued for a dynamic rather than static criterion; in other words, a principle that tolerates inequalities but tries to use them in the context of social partnership. I know the welfare state has more or less been built around the anti-poverty struggle. As valuable as it is, this objective can also be harmful, since it allows us to maintain inequalities without any reciprocity between the rich and the poor.[59]

The paradox of a BI is that, by giving to everyone, it is the weakest who benefit the most. Such a paradox, however, is easily cleared up in recognizing the policy's heavily progressive distributive structure. In light of this situation and the four constraints we talked about above, the only acceptable answer to the question regarding the ideal level for a BI is "as high as possible," since it is at this benefit level, and this level only, that we give priority to the interests of the most disadvantaged in society. This concern for social partnership has to guide us in any important decisions regarding the future of the welfare state. Our society will be just when economic and social policies, particularly a BI, are arranged so that they cannot be changed without undermining, at least for a while, the situation of the most disadvantaged.

* * *

There is no pre-established harmony between efficiency and fairness, but, as I have said, these values are not necessarily opposed to one another and while we may not be able to reconcile them completely, we can at least bring them closer together than they are today. Meanwhile, we have to remember that in situations of conflict, justice should always have priority over efficiency. Rapid economic and technological changes require that we define forms of social partnership that are more flexible and better adjusted to the new social and economic realities. We need measures that do not discourage individual initiative and that increase everyone's chances of having some form of useful activity in areas as diverse as leisure, knowledge, environmental protection and care for others.

Liberals have reason to emphasize the advances that have contributed to the wealth of capitalist organizations. Our societies have made huge conquests economically, scientifically and socially; however they still tolerate huge economic inequalities between their citizens. This is not a new phenomenon; inequalities existed before the emergence of capitalism. The problem we have today is how to effectively fight against what we consider to be the most unjustifiable inequalities, while preserving as far as possible our standard of living and our environment for future generations.

A BI will make wealth redistribution easier, more transparent and, eventually, more generous. It will also do a much better job of responding to the needs of social justice than the selective and stigmatizing programs that we introduced at the end of the 1960s, thinking that they would serve only a marginal part of the population. The proposal does not constitute the only solution to our troubles, but it deserves its place today among the few serious alternatives for getting the contemporary welfare state out of its dead-end situation. We now have to take a look at how we can implement it over the short term.

3
Achieving a Basic Income Starting Now

The challenges of change

We can achieve a Basic Income. Obviously, as with any change of this magnitude, we will need patience, imagination and discipline. There is no real difficulty in implementing a redistributive measure that is much simpler and more coherent than other measures. The main challenge is in substituting it, as gently as possible and without creating too many administrative, financial and economic setbacks, for the myriad of poorly integrated indirect (personal income tax) and direct (the various means of income security) benefits. Many of these benefits will eventually become redundant, but for now, they ensure necessary financial protection during the transition period leading up to a universal program.

In the world today, numerous scenarios for financing and instituting a BI are being looked at.[1] In Canada, an important investigative body, the MacDonald Commission, suggested to the federal government in 1985 that it reform income security in favour of a unified benefit.[2] The Commission concluded that the Canadian income security plan at the time was "ineffective," "complex" and "unjust" and that it needed major reform.[3] The proposal for an unconditional Basic Income for every citizen was more or less well received by social policy analysts, but it raised some strong opposition from the Canadian Left, which unequivocally associated the MacDonald Commission's collective recommendations with a neo-conservative mindset.[4] A year later, another Canadian investigative body, the Forget Commission on Unemployment Insurance, picked up the MacDonald Commission's proposal.[5] The majority report was attacked outright by the Left, particularly by unions, which refused to accept the proposed substantial cuts to unemployment insurance benefits. The time has come to pick up the trail where it was left off and pursue it to the end, while clearly defining the goals of a BI along the way. I am increasingly convinced that if Canada had taken the path laid out by the MacDonald Commission in 1985, we would not have such a high number of people, and particularly children, in poverty today. We would also have preserved the universality of certain programs, such as family allowance. Let us hope that there is still time to change tracks and resume the initiative for change.

Preliminary thoughts on costs

Evaluating the cost of a measure such as a BI depends on several factors. Universality can come into it, but not necessarily. We have to constantly keep this in mind, because one of the deepest-held beliefs today is that universal measures invariably cost more than targeted measures, which redistribute only to those in need. If this belief were well founded, the per capita cost for health care in Canada would necessarily be higher than it is in the United States. We know that this is not the case. We therefore have to avoid automatically associating universality with extravagance.

The most common mistake made by BI detractors (and even some of its supporters!) is confusing the gross amount of the policy's benefits (the value of the benefit multiplied by the number of citizens) and the net amount (the gross amount minus the savings made by eliminating various income security programs and reorganizing the tax structure). This quickly leads to astronomical figures that are not at all realistic. Instituting a BI will require substantial changes to the welfare state as we know it. We can do this by gradually replacing social assistance programs that do not work well or that will simply no longer have a reason to exist once a BI is in place. What will be the extent of such changes? There is no single answer to this question. In some cases, the need to replace a particular program will be obvious, but other possible substitutions will inevitably raise controversy. This is certainly understandable. Many of our citizens depend totally or partially on social assistance programs and it is normal for them to worry about seeing them replaced with a new measure that they are not familiar with. The extent of the substitutions is a crucial variable in evaluating cost. I will come back to this later in this chapter.

A look at two complementary notions

We need to determine what we mean by "cost." There are at least two complementary notions: (i) budgetary cost, in other words, the share of government funds required to fund this measure; and (ii) the cost for households, in other words the effect on the disposable income of persons or families following the reorganization that would result from implementing an unconditional income. Understandably, the distributive variable of a social assistance policy is just as important as the strictly budgetary variable, which does not differentiate between taxpayers.[6] It is important to have an idea of who the winners and losers are with this kind of measure. A resource reallocation of this magnitude cannot be achieved without any cost to taxpayers, although we can minimize some of the effects through various ad hoc adjustments. To succeed, we need to compare the effects of this financial reallocation on each group in society (individuals, youth, couples, parents, wage earners, pensioners and so on) and determine what is appropriate for the middle and long terms.

To implement a BI, we always have to keep the two costs in mind: budgetary cost and the cost for each category of taxpayers. This is not terribly difficult in itself, but to measure these costs accurately, we need to conduct budgetary simulations using databases and software that are not accessible to everyone. We also have to draw conclusions from the fact that these two notions remain globally independent from one another. Let us look at an example: It is entirely possible to achieve a BI with a zero budgetary cost for the government, but it would then need to be financed through a major disruption of household income and by further tapping into the income of a large part of the population. In theory, this could work, but before putting it into practice we would need to look at the many serious issues associated with it. Although a BI may well be a good idea, we need to give everyone enough time to prepare themselves for changes that could affect their disposable incomes. Poorly monitored distributional effects could cause considerable harm to those who have contracted liabilities in good faith and who must now adjust to a new fiscal and financial environment.[7]

Why does a Basic Income cost more?

Before discussing some implementation scenarios, I would like to set out the factors explaining why this type of proposal would necessarily be more expensive than the status quo. In fact, there are two main factors, which are only indirectly linked to the principle of universality.

The first factor behind an inevitable cost increase: we need to devote extra money to individualizing the current welfare scheme. Right now, last resort payments such as social assistance benefits are provided to households and not individuals, which is contrary to the individualization rule governing a BI. In concrete terms, a household with one individual would receive a benefit amounting to approximately $500. As soon as there are at least two recipients living together in the same residence, however, each of them has their payment cut by about $100. Our governments believe there are economies of scale in the fixed costs of sharing a residence. They feel that this authorizes them to reduce the amount of each recipient's benefit. This unfortunate practice ends up hindering mutual aid and cooperation among those who need it the most. It also requires civil servants to monitor household status which, aside from becoming increasingly complicated considering the range of current lifestyles, forces them to immerse themselves in the private lives of recipients. As I said in Chapter 2, individualizing social assistance benefits and the tax system would be efficient and just. With or without a BI, we will have to do this eventually in order to ensure greater independence for everyone and to encourage mobility and responsibility. Most other benefits, such as unemployment insurance benefits and Old Age Security, are already individualized. The same thing has to happen with social assistance. For Quebec only, it was calculated that such a measure would increase social assistance by 200 million dollars in 1998. This is obviously a lot of money, but with the program's total social assistance budget of 3.3 million, this change would represent a proportion of barely 6 per cent. I assume that the proportion would be the same for other Canadian provinces.

The second factor requiring a budget increase is the most decisive, yet also the most difficult to grasp on an intuitive level. It pertains to the fundamental goal of getting recipients out of the poverty trap. I will try to illustrate it here with a simple example.

Let us suppose that, convinced that social assistance stigmatizes people and dissuades them from getting paid work, our governments agree to provide a benefit without any repayment conditions to current recipients. These recipients can then keep this income and concurrently draw other income that is taxed similarly to the incomes of all citizens, rather than the close to 100 per cent rate that is currently in place. What would such a measure represent in terms of additional cost to governmental budgets? At first glance, nothing, or almost nothing. In fact, these sums of money are already being allocated and the deduction for recipients declaring employment earnings is just as small. That explains why many of those eligible for social assistance say they do not understand what the government gains by taxing their incomes in this way. The reason is more structural than financial.

Making social assistance into an amount that can be drawn at the same time as paid income would substantially boost the situation of social assistance recipients compared to the working poor. This would create tax situations that would make no sense at all in terms of justice or the economy. In Quebec, to use an example in dollars and cents, a full-time worker receiving the minimum wage has a net income of approximately $1,000 per month once all the tax and other deductions have been made. This is roughly twice as much as what a social assistance recipient living alone receives. Such a gap can still motivate people to keep their jobs. But if we allow recipients to keep their entire allowance and then receive wages on top of that without any penalty, then they would only have to work half the amount of time as workers to receive the same monthly income. This is obviously unjust as well as impossible to manage. Workers would feel compelled to sign up for social assistance right away in order to have the same advantages as recipients. If necessary, they would reduce their time at work, thereby getting caught up in the vicious cycle of the poverty trap, which is central to the whole issue.

The problem is not in providing the non-working population money that they are already receiving anyway. The difficulty is that if we allow this segment of the population to collect additional income at a tax rate similar to that of the working population, then we need to simultaneously increase the net income of the latter to ensure that they still have an advantage in working. Does this mean that, in order to institute a BI, we will have to increase everyone's income? If by "income" we mean collective earnings before tax, then yes: all citizens would have the same Basic Income from the government. But if we are talking strictly about net income, or after-tax income, the improvements agreed upon for the poorest groups would decrease progressively in accordance with the tax-back rate, which remains to be determined (this rate obviously represents a crucial variable in determining BI costs.) Starting at a certain income level, this "income-effect" will mean that the more fortunate taxpayers will no longer get any additional monetary benefit from a BI; they will actually find themselves financing some of it. This transformation is the inevitable price to pay in decreasing the overly high tax bite suffered by the non-working population, while increasing the net income of the poorest citizens.

How much would this tax adjustment cost the citizens who have to foot the bill for higher tax rates? That depends on several factors, including the structure of the new tax tables. The budgetary effort would not be insignificant. It would, however, have the virtue of creating a much more coherent indirect and direct benefit system with a much stronger work incentive for disadvantaged groups.

Since we now know the two new budgetary constraints to take into consideration in achieving a BI in the short term, let us try and identify the means at our disposal to tackle them.

Various funding options to explore

We now can agree that distributing a BI, compared to distributing social assistance, for example, would necessarily require an additional budgetary effort. This effort supports two fundamental contemporary social policy objectives: (i) individualizing benefits (to put an end to household investigations); and (ii) better integration of taxation and benefits (to eliminate the tax trap of current recipients and increase the net income of the working poor). These are worthy objectives and it is unfortunate that we have waited so long before taking any action on them.

BI supporters have proposed several funding solutions. I will only present the best known of these in this section. I will also explain why these options are less than perfect and sometimes even unacceptable. I know full well that this will be a minefield for debate. There is certainly not just one single way of achieving a BI; no pre-determined, consensus-building route to take. I feel that a progressive approach is better and certainly more realistic, both politically and economically as well as on the budgetary front. I will tell you why in the following sections, but let us start by examining certain funding strategies that regularly have been espoused.

Relying on an increase of business activity and on savings generated by simplifying bureaucracy

We can deny a BI would cost more than the status quo by emphasizing the enormous social costs currently being generated by society's poor. Current programs contribute to the social and economic exclusion of a significant part of the population that no longer has an interest in working or in receiving better training. Is it therefore not conceivable that the social and economic revitalization associated with a generous benefit could finance the additional costs for the general population? Think about the new tax income that would be generated by a return to the workforce of millions of people or the savings in social program administration. Should we not view the initial money that we put toward a significant BI as an investment that would quickly generate enough earnings to finance itself?[8]

We can certainly hope for this, while remaining cautious when it comes time to account for these new savings. A substantial BI would inevitably lead to significant adjustments in the behaviour of economic agents. Some of these adjustments would benefit society as a whole, but the size of this benefit would be difficult to measure with any accuracy.[9] For example, as long as we have adequate wage policies, a BI would be an incentive for many non-working poor to return to work. Would this be enough for the measure to finance itself? No one can say for sure, since the economy is too imprecise a science to make these kinds of forecasts. We also have to consider the possible negative effects on consumption, moonlighting activity, the demand for training, the participation rate of middle-income households, the debt level of individuals and so on. A substantial BI, for example, could undermine the incentive to work for households that already have two employment incomes, especially when one of these is particularly low.[10] For this reason and others, to rely solely on economic growth to finance the measure's additional costs does not seem reasonable, even less so if we believe that the measure must increasingly be designed to bear in mind environmental protection and the right of future generations to a standard of living that is comparable to our own.

Giving only to those who are "truly in need"

To decrease BI costs, we could consider withdrawing one or more of its three unconditionality rules. Many adopt this approach, believing that complete universality could still be achieved eventually, once certain features have been partially put into place. Things are not that simple, however, and the foreseen savings could be insignificant, if not non-existent. To help us understand, let us remember the triple unconditionality feature in question.

A BI is revenue that is provided:

- irrespective of any means-tested evidence (cumulative rule);
- irrespective of the income of other household members (individualization rule); and,
- irrespective of a work requirement or a commitment to hold a job or to receive some form of training (freedom of choice rule).

I will start with the first "cumulative" rule. We now know that the goal of providing a BI to everyone is not to increase everyone's net income, which would not make sense, but to achieve a better integration of benefits and taxation. If this is the case, then why not simply give only "to those who really need it, workers included"? In this way, social assistance recipients would continue to receive financial aid set at a minimum amount but the difference from today is that they would be able to keep a portion of their employment income. They could then be subjected to a different tax-back rate, say one dollar for each two dollars of employment income (equalling a marginal rate of 50 per cent). The working poor would also have the right to a supplement calculated at the end of each fiscal year. This supplement could be paid in advance on a monthly basis, as is already the case, for example, with the Guaranteed Income Supplement for seniors in Canada. At a certain level of declared income, of course, a worker would no longer receive this supplement. He or she would therefore become a "net taxpayer" in the eyes of the tax and social assistance systems. The tax/benefit integration for these two population categories would therefore have been achieved without seriously affecting the income of other taxpayers and without the huge influx of money needed to achieve a BI.

The proposal to allow social assistance recipients to keep a decreasing portion of their work earnings and poor workers to receive a decreasing supplement to encourage them to keep their jobs is called a negative income tax. Today, it constitutes the most serious alternative to a BI. In France, for example, it is getting some attention from the Parti socialiste.[11]

Negative income taxation has often been associated, wrongly in my opinion, with a regressive social policy — a prejudice that has existed from its inception. In fact, the concept was defended about thirty years ago by the neo-conservative Nobel Laureate in economics, Milton Friedman, who, as we know, never missed an opportunity to criticize the welfare state or social democracy.[12] We would be wrong, however, to stop there in evaluating the proposal's merits. In fact, all things being equal, the negative tax and the BI are two sides of the same coin. They allow us to achieve objectives that are largely similar with respect to redistributing wealth and integrating taxation with social assistance (refer to Appendix A, where I compare their distributional structures). The principle of an employment income supplement has already been realized in several countries, including Canada, but it is generally targeted to a very specific clientele of poor households with children and at least one employment income.[13] A negative income tax would generalize this form of indirect subsidy to employment incomes by replacing current programs, which is also the case with a BI. The important issue now is whether the negative income tax can be considered a solution that is truly less expensive than a BI.

What is clear and seems to bode in favour of the negative income tax is that such a tax prevents the government from paying out astronomical amounts of money, a good portion of which is automatically reimbursed through tax systems. Many people who support the general objectives of a BI are opposed to the "nonsense" of distributing benefits to a segment of the population that does not have any need for it. The negative income tax avoids this paradoxical and, perhaps, embarrassing situation. But is it simpler to manage or any less expensive? Not really.

Since the negative income tax and BI proposals are entirely symmetrical, they necessarily involve identical budgetary costs (same effect on individualizing benefits, reducing the effective marginal tax rate of non-workers and increasing the net income of the working poor). Naturally, the necessary expenditures are very different since a BI provides as an advance that which the negative tax reimburses following a means test. As I said earlier, a BI would have a much greater effect on tax rates than the negative income tax, and I admit that this is a variable that must be considered and which could work against a BI. But contrary to what is generally affirmed, even by some social policy experts, a BI and a negative income tax lead to budgetary costs that are strictly identical. So, why choose a BI?

Essentially because the negative income tax formula, despite its real advantages compared to the status quo, is poorly suited to the needs of the disadvantaged, who have insecure jobs and who often go from being employed to unemployed in a short period of time. These people are in a precarious economic situation and we simply cannot let their fear of risk or change escalate.[14] Many of the disadvantaged, who normally could hold a small job and receive an additional supplement, do not do it today because they are afraid that the transition would be too difficult and that if they fail, the benefit they are entitled to would not be provided in time. The government therefore forces the neediest in society to jump through endless administrative hoops and to finance for themselves an advance on the money that will ultimately be reimbursed to them anyway — a rather illogical attitude to take!

Naturally, benefits must adapt to fluctuations in employment income, but personal income tax is much better suited to this since it applies to real, and not foreseen, earnings. This is particularly important for those with uncertain job prospects, who are repeatedly told that they must take more risks on the job market and who furthermore have to face bureaucratic delays.[15] Status as a full-time recipient provides at least the advantage of a modest, stable income without the inevitable administrative hassles of a negative income tax.

With a BI, there are no bureaucratic delays and there is no uncertainty and no humiliation. The maximum benefit is automatically given to all and the amount never varies, whatever our choices or mistakes. The burden of proof is even reversed in favour of the most disadvantaged, since it is the wealthiest who have to prove in their income tax returns that the onus is not on them to completely finance this unconditional income.

In Canada, the MacDonald Commission understood that these two formulas would engender identical costs for the government. Considering the ease of management and transparency of a BI and the nation's social policy customs, it preferred a BI to the negative income tax.

Not individualizing transfers

If providing income *ex post*, through a supplement, rather than *ex ante*, through an advance, does not change the costs of a BI in any way, then maybe we should look at the second unconditionality requirement: individualization. We established above that such a policy would necessarily generate costs for the government in making the system fairer to individual cohabitants. Should we continue nonetheless to provide household benefits for a certain period of time? I do not think so, although I acknowledge that this would provide real economic savings as opposed to what we would have with the negative income tax. Three reasons lead me to reject the idea of maintaining household benefits. First, as I already mentioned, individualizing both direct and indirect benefits seems to me to be inevitable and highly desirable, if only to avoid all the administrative hassles and the infringement on people's privacy.

Second, it is better to start individualizing sooner, since the required effort will be less. If we wait, for example, until we have achieved a relatively higher level of a BI before implementing this individualization, we will need even more money than today, the resistance to change will be stronger and the redistributive effects more questionable, because individualizing benefits necessarily improves the relative situation of couples as opposed to individuals living alone. This seems to be an inevitable outcome, however, if we consider current reductions for cohabitants as unjustified and counterproductive.

My third reason for not postponing individualization is that it does not constitute the largest cost of a BI. It is financially more demanding to reduce the effective marginal tax rate of social assistance recipients and increase the net earnings of the working poor. This is why I recommend that we keep on course with individualization and look elsewhere for conceivable savings or less difficult implementation scenarios.

Requiring a consideration in exchange for a guaranteed income

A BI should normally be provided without a work requirement or a commitment to register in a training program (freedom of choice rule). We hope to increase everyone's ability to determine what best suits them by offering them more resources than they have today. While condemning workfare, certain BI supporters have convinced themselves that on economic as well as political grounds, we should at least attach this basic benefit to an obligation to participate in a "socially useful" activity, thereby creating a type of participation income.[16]

The definition of what is "socially useful" naturally remains ambiguous. If we are not careful, we could find ourselves slipping toward a form of workfare that is incompatible with the spirit of a BI. Generally, proponents of a participation income are trying to ease their way into a BI, since it appears the general population is not yet ready for a radically unconditional measure. As a means of countering such resistance, therefore, they recommend the benefit be tied to a series of social contributions that are not too constraining, such as looking after children or persons needing support, holding or actively looking for a paid job, getting some training or taking courses, volunteering for a recognized organization, helping community businesses, and so on. The main logic behind participation income is that each citizen who wants support from the government must show a willingness to get off this support eventually or a desire to do something positive for the community.

For purely strategic reasons, this might be the best way to implement a BI.[17] We have to admit, however, that our financing problem would not be resolved. In fact, even the main supporters of participation income generally acknowledge that by introducing rules of conditionality to a policy that is intended to be universal, we are adding considerable control measures that could end up costing more than an unconditional benefit. Furthermore, by implementing participation income, we run the risk of moving toward a purely bureaucratic definition and control of what are "socially useful activities." In my opinion, this is taking place right now with the social or community-based economy. Unfortunately, government intervention in these areas progressively undermines the purpose of such spontaneous practices as volunteerism and mutual aid.

Broadening the tax base

If changing the unconditional structure of a BI does not generate significant savings, at least not enough to finance it entirely, should we then take the bull by the horns and increase disposable income by broadening the tax base? Many suggestions deserve to be looked at: an elimination of tax shelters of questionable benefit, a higher tax on luxury items, ecological taxes, taxation of worldwide financial transfers, advertising taxes, higher consumption and inheritance taxes, implementation of a capital tax at a single fixed rate worldwide to counter tax competition between governments, an adjustment of capital tax so that it approaches the income tax rate, flat tax on gross revenue, a more direct redistribution of public corporation earnings and so on. None of these suggestions should be dismissed out of hand, because it is just as important to renew our thinking on how to best extract wealth fairly and efficiently as it is on how to redistribute it. These two goals are fundamentally complementary and even though I have devoted myself entirely to the latter in this work, I am thoroughly convinced that we are not doing enough today to achieve either goal because we have not known how to adapt to the numerous structural upheavals in our economy.

That said, I still have important reservations on linking together at all costs the short-term achievement of a BI with a broadening of the tax base. First, we increase the difficulties as well as the opportunities for resistance with a measure that is already politically controversial and whose fiercest opponents come from the Left as much as they do the Right. Second, and in my opinion most decisive, this strategy is not best from a public management point of view. An increase in government revenues or the rationalization of its expenses will always be on the agenda, with or without a BI. Instead, we need to move step by step, starting with relatively simple substitutions that have the potential for building a sizable consensus. We could then progressively increase the benefit to significant levels. A sudden implementation would cause radical changes in the division of household income and would unduly favour couples compared to individuals. This may well be a desirable consequence of individualizing benefits and integrating them with taxation, but we still have to protect the lowest incomes during this transition period. Once the majority of citizens have felt the benefits of the proposed changes and have learned to recognize certain fundamental principles such as the right to a strictly unconditional Basic Income that is cumulative and individualized, then opposition predicated solely on bias will hopefully decrease. We will know then that these changes are beneficial for society as a whole and for present and future generations. A BI, like any policy, has to prove itself.

Starting with a partial allowance

Like many BI supporters in the world today, I feel that the best way to institute this measure is to start off with a limited amount, set below the current social assistance level.[18] A full allowance, in other words a benefit that entirely replaces the current Social Assistance Program, is not a good idea, at least not temporarily. In the first place, it would be rather expensive on the budgetary front, although this wouldn't be the main difficulty (it is always possible to challenge certain government expenses, particularly subsidies to corporations and personal tax shelters). A full allowance would cause a major disruption of household income and this could have negative repercussions on economic activity (prohibitive tax rates, strong redistribution of income from individuals to couples, sudden increase in marginal rates for low-income workers, risk of a decrease in demand for work in certain job categories and so on). I do not think we should be taking so many risks when the people with the most to lose are those with the lowest incomes.

Like many BI supporters, I therefore suggest we do not solely rely on fundamental changes in government income sources to implement the measure in the short term. Instead, I suggest that we take the initial but necessary step of doing more with the money we already have. This approach, as well as being more economically and politically prudent, will not prevent us from ensuring that the measure grows quickly in the second stage. On the contrary, it will be that much easier, since the effort to implement the new structure will be that much less.

I realize that a partial rather than full BI perplexes many people, and particularly disappoints those who battle against poverty on a daily basis and who have been demanding an increase in social assistance levels for years. These social assistance levels, remember, are largely below the lowest-income cut-offs. If a BI is trying to be more successful than current programs, should it not logically at least meet these cut-offs? What could $250 or $300 per adult per month do against poverty and exclusion? Much more than you might think.

Since a partial BI will allow us to implement a completely different distribution mechanism from what we have right now, its benefits will normally be felt right away. I will explain how in the following section. The important thing to grasp is that we need to open up new avenues and that increasing social assistance is not a viable solution, since this will create a greater number of recipients with an ever greater dependency, as we saw in Chapter 1. The welfare state has reached a dead end as a result of a host of interrelated problems: inadequate income of workers and non-workers alike, of course, but also work disincentive, incoherent implicit and explicit marginal tax rates, dependency on benefits with respect to the wage structure, non-individualization of social assistance benefits and so on. A BI tackles each of these, but it cannot resolve overnight that which we have ignored for years. Once the structural difficulties have been ironed out, our ultimate objective to eradicate poverty will again become a possibility: right now, with the means currently at our disposal, this is completely out of our grasp.[19]

The inadequacy of non-workers' incomes is just one of the aspects leading to poverty and exclusion, and it cannot be separated from other difficulties that are just as serious but that, until now, have only received the attention of experts.

Short-term implementation scenario

A BI that is modest yet sufficient to create a new dynamic favouring the most disadvantaged could be financed rather easily by eliminating the following programs:

- Family allowance and collective child benefits
- Tax credit for dependent children
- Personal tax credit
- Spousal tax credit
- Tax credits for federal and provincial consumption taxes
- Guaranteed Income Supplement for seniors
- Old Age Security
- The portion of social assistance formally distributed through a form of universal allowance.

A modest yet individualized, tax-free and cumulative benefit

The above list is not necessarily exhaustive. In fact, I am deliberately presenting a proposal that roughly resembles that of the MacDonald Commission in order to re-use some of their numerical data.[20] Other, more radical implementation scenarios are conceivable, such as the immediate elimination of collective social insurance programs (other tax credits, employment insurance, tax shelters for group or private pension plans) and student loan and grant programs, but this would create difficulties in the short term that I will come back to later.[21] For now, however, we will illustrate this proposal with some examples and point out the main stumbling blocks to avoid, but it is certainly a scenario that can work.

Eliminating the personal tax credit would have the immediate effect of stretching the tax base to the first dollar earned. To compensate, each citizen would receive a reimbursable personal tax credit that would be distributed periodically — basically a BI in its embryonic form. Contrary to what we would expect, such a measure does not end up being fiscally neutral. In fact, very low income earners would benefit, since current tax credits only represent a potential gain for sole taxpayers. Making this credit reimbursable has the immediate effect of sharing its fiscal value with a larger number of people.

Of course, not all of the recommended substitutions have such a wonderful distributional result. Replacing targeted programs (benefits for children, social assistance recipients and seniors) would have negative consequences in that we would be paying to everyone that which had previously been reserved for society's poor. We would therefore inevitably have to modify the tax structure in order to recover these benefits recurrently. If we want to get rid of all these conditional programs and replace them with a single, simplified and transparent plan — and we do need to do this — then in return we have to increase tax rates on the highest incomes to absorb their equivalent in disposable income and achieve the expected distributional results. This is neither complicated nor unusual. The tax system has a redistributive role and it is normal, even necessary in many cases, to adapt it in accordance with changes to the benefits awarded directly to individuals.

Some revealing figures

The MacDonald Commission calculated that its proposal for a universal income security scheme would have provided $3,825 in 1984 to all adults under sixty-five (a little less for children and more for seniors). Today, this benefit would total more than $6,000, which is enough to entirely replace social assistance for one person. To partially finance this reform, commission members suggested that the federal government withdraw completely from its joint financing of social assistance (around 50 per cent at the time). They invited provinces, however, to maintain their contribution level in the form of a supplement to the federal benefit. I calculated that, in 1998 dollars, a family of four without any other income would have received a total of between $19,375 and $20,925 in federal and provincial allowances. This might not seem like a lot, but it is much more than what this same family receives today. If such a level of benefit were available universally and cumulatively, there would be a significant effect on poverty. In fact, there would likely be two times fewer poor people in Canada, since half of them already depend on employment income and they would all have something to gain by receiving a cumulative supplement of this kind.

As well as being relatively generous compared to what was being offered at the time, the MacDonald proposal was extremely progressive fiscally. In fact, commission members had anticipated a rather slow tax-back rate of 20 per cent, which allowed a higher number of households to benefit from the reform. In concrete terms, families with two children and an income of less than $46,500 in 1998 ($30,000 in 1985) would have had a net increase over the former system. This relative generosity, however, had a price attached, since well-off families with an income of more than $77,500 could have paid up to $7,750 more per year. The affluent classes therefore needed to bear a large part of the costs of this reform. Aware of this burden, the Commission decided it would be a good idea to prepare a second, less-redistributive, and likely more politically acceptable scenario.[22]

The figures above give us a certain sense of scale. We still need to see more accurate figures with effects on tax rates, poverty and inequality. Based on some summary calculations that I have seen, however, it would be conceivable to finance a BI without overly disrupting household incomes, at a level of $300 per month for individuals or $3,600 per year and $7,200 per couple. This completely tax-free allowance would be added to other disposable incomes. This proposal more or less resembles ones currently being considered in other countries, notably Great Britain, Belgium, Finland, the Netherlands and Ireland.[23] It constitutes a very conservative working hypothesis that would not really increase government expenses. After all, it has the great advantage of attacking the current tax structure all at once and preparing the groundwork for increased benefits. I do not think that there is any other option that could do as well in the short term.

My proposal does not take into consideration the savings in managing programs. Neither does it consider the positive effects on economic activity that could increase the benefit level. It does, however, account for the fact that social assistance will continue in the form of a supplement and that it will be paid out during the transition period in order to guarantee the total current income of those eligible. Let us now take a look at the potential consequences of such a benefit.

Progressively relinquishing non-workers from the poverty trap

Improving the situation of current social assistance recipients has to be done through a draconian decrease in their marginal effective tax rate and not through an increase in social assistance, which would only serve to exclude them more. Increasing their social assistance at a time when we are reducing their tax rate would create a system that would work completely against them, causing them to retreat further into dependency. The priority for this group should be to provide them with a full allowance as soon as possible, but between now and then, a partial BI would give them options that they do not have now. In fact, every dollar in conditional benefits that we succeed in converting into a dollar of BI represents one more step toward dismantling the poverty trap.

To illustrate the above, I will take the simple example of a single person who currently receives an average of $500 in social assistance payments per month. According to my working hypothesis, this person would receive a BI of $300 and a social assistance supplement of $200. What could this do to change his or her situation? A lot more than we could ever imagine.

First, some recipients will quit social assistance for good since they can already count on a declared monthly employment income that is equal to or more than $200. Others that have undeclared employment income would no longer risk moonlighting for a residual benefit of $200, especially if declared employment gives them access to protective social measures that they are not entitled to right now. We know that the best way to combat moonlighting in this fraction of the population is to decrease their effective marginal tax rate, which is currently set at 100 per cent. By substituting, even partially, a non-taxable allowance for their current benefit, we reduce their effective tax rate accordingly. This is essential for the eventual recovery of benefits for this segment of the population. A partial BI allows us to get there, slowly but surely.

Recipients with no employment income can also greatly benefit from having their social assistance gradually replaced with a BI. Today, recipients need an employment income of $500 per month or more to be able to quit social assistance. With a BI of $300 per month, they need only $200 in employment income to end their dependency on social assistance. It is a step toward freedom for all those in the poverty trap who feel they can find a small paid job at this level. A more substantial BI will decrease the penalty proportionately and will ultimately transform the current poverty trap into a launching pad for all kinds of productive activities.

Couples or individuals sharing housing and receiving social assistance would benefit even more. Right now, a childless couple receives approximately $775 per month in social assistance. With a partial and individualized BI, this couple will receive a total of $600. Since they have to maintain their current income, social assistance would have to give them $175 ($775 minus $600). This works out well for them, since to leave social assistance for good, this couple will only have to find an income of $175 per month, which is much more accessible than an employment income of $775. The individualization of benefits that began with a BI would make poor working and non-working couples the direct winners of this reform (a predictable, and some say paradoxical, result of individualization).

Increasing the net income of the working population

With this type of scenario, the non-working population benefits primarily from new possibilities brought about by lower taxes on their employment earnings. The situation of the working poor is understandably different. Remember that this group constitutes half of the poor people in Canada. An allowance as modest as $300 at an acceptable tax-back rate will benefit households that are already close to the critical thresholds of poverty. According to economic and social logic, the first to get out of poverty will therefore be the working poor, whose total incomes are closest to the poverty line. As we know, the problem they face day after day is not so much their marginal tax rate as the small gap that separates them from non-workers. An unconditional allowance of $300 will be a gain that is added to their employment income. This will encourage them to keep their jobs, without ever forcing them to do so. Some of them, particularly two-income households that are hovering around the poverty line, will never again be part of the poverty statistics.

As for economically dependent persons, especially women, young people and seniors, they will now be able to count on an unconditional income that will be small at the start, but that will make them progressively less dependent on their spouse, parents or children respectively. Consistent with the freedom of choice rule, no one should be trapped in a social category against their will.

Decreasing net income for some and increasing marginal tax rates for others

We can easily make these improvements by reallocating available resources. However, one cannot make an omelette without breaking eggs first. Within the confines of budget neutrality and a static framework, any gain for one group necessarily ends in a net loss for another group. In the case of the scenario I am defending here, it is the more affluent categories of the population who will inevitably experience a marked decrease in their indirect and direct benefits. This is the price to pay for further harmonizing taxation with benefits without undermining the situation of the most disadvantaged.

Low-income earners must also expect more than a small increase in their marginal tax rates. This is obviously not ideal, but it is difficult to institute a BI any other way. The problem is basically structural: a decrease in the indirect marginal tax rates of non-workers has the consequence, in both the short and long terms, of increasing the direct marginal tax rates of the disadvantaged working population. Remember that a BI, partial or not, replaces current personal tax credits with a monetary benefit. All disposable income therefore becomes entirely taxable. This tax transformation is most troubling for low-income earners. In fact, since the relative value of the current tax credit is greater for people earning $15,000 than it is for people earning $50,000, an equally higher proportion of the income of the first group becomes taxable again. Of course, introducing a BI results in a net gain that entirely compensates for this increase in the marginal tax rate. However, it does not prevent it from doubling, and we can see how this segment of the population might find it tempting to moonlight. This tax transformation seems inevitable, at least over the long term. It allows us to bring the marginal tax rates of all societal groups closer together while maintaining the desired progressiveness of average rates across income brackets (once the BI has been provided, of course).

A partial BI allows us to reduce the effects of such a fiscal transformation, which would be much worse with a full BI.[24] However, if necessary, we can reduce its effects by broadening the tax base, which could further help the low-income groups by financing the BI in a way that would leave a portion of personal tax credits in place.

Is a Basic Income politically realistic?

If we simply stick to the amounts of money we have used up until now, then a BI is realistic. But it is often pointed out to me that such major changes would require exemplary cooperation between the federal and provincial levels of government. There is some doubt, in the current Canadian political context, whether our politicians and institutions would be up for such a collaborative effort. What should we do in such a case? One solution, envisioned by the MacDonald Commission, is to make BI a federal responsibility. This could be done by using resources currently being dispersed by programs that will be replaced, including federal transfer payments to the provinces for social assistance. The amount of the benefit should normally resemble that obtained in the preceding scenario. Each Canadian citizen will therefore have an amount paid unconditionally that is completely tax-free and that can be cumulated with other support income — in particular, conditional supplements that the provinces will fund themselves. Such a policy would allow us to maintain the equalization function of the wealthy provinces toward the poorer provinces. Obviously, however, nothing prevents a province, territory or even a region from implementing such a policy. In fact, the first government in the world to have offered all its citizens a BI is Alaska, which still uses this mechanism today to distribute a share of its oil profits.[25]

As for the politicians, we have to make their job easier when it comes to defending such a reform. The most serious critics of a BI stress its prohibitive cost. This objection is well justified if we are looking for a tool that will completely eradicate poverty overnight. A partial BI, to which conditional benefits will be attached throughout the transition period, offers a more realistic solution, while at the same time changing the way we achieve social partnership. There is increasing consensus among BI supporters on the importance of a gradual implementation. More radical implementation methods are also proposed in the literature, but they demand either a monetary creation,[26] with the inflationary pressures that go along with it, or inflated tax revenues, which I do not reject on principle but mainly because they are unrealistic on a budgetary and political level. The method suggested here avoids these extreme positions since it basically involves reallocating resources that are already in circulation. By instituting a BI gradually, we keep the principle of unconditionality totally intact, which does the most over the long term to change today's antiquated attitudes regarding social assistance. Once the process is well under way, we can ask ourselves what we have to do to finance a higher level of guaranteed income. A number of options will be open to us because, in the early stages of implementation, we have not changed much with respect to current income distribution and the way in which income is tapped. In the following section, I will present some of the potential outcomes of implementing a BI in our social security system. Like many others, I firmly believe that a BI will be at the heart of reform proposals in twenty-first century social policy. And now is the time to begin getting ready.

The future of a Basic Income and the welfare state

There are not many realistic alternatives to a BI that can claim a similar reconciliation of justice and efficiency. Aside from the negative income tax, which, despite its advantages, presents obvious drawbacks for the disadvantaged, there are few strategies to combat the crisis in the welfare state.

Economic recovery? The gross national product (GNP) has continued to increase over the last few years and this has had relatively little effect on the number of those who are poor and excluded. As we have seen in times of relative prosperity, economic growth alone does not eradicate poverty and unemployment. In fact, the opposite is sometimes true, when business profits are automatically reinvested in new machinery that allows us to produce more with fewer people.

Decrease in work hours? This would not help much, particularly if coercive legislation is introduced that treats all job categories alike. This ends up being costly for the community as a whole and carries the risk of inefficiency and job losses. A more intelligent way to encourage job sharing is to finance leisure time by providing income that is independent from work. Workers could more easily reduce their time at work to devote themselves to personal fulfillment. The BI would therefore serve as an instrument to promote work sharing.

Government funding of new jobs?[27] We are already doing a lot of this and in many different ways: support to private enterprise; hiring in the public sector; subsidies for activities that are deemed to be "socially economic"; support to artists, farmers, remote areas, business start-ups, specific categories of unemployed or social assistant recipients and so on. We can always do more, but international competition might well call us to order soon. Out of a concern for transparency, we can no longer finance jobs like we do today, in response to circumstances, government priorities or pure electoral opportunism. By targeting subsidies to different job categories, we end up with numerous unwanted effects, such as unfair competition between jobs or job sectors and the increased risk of inefficiency. We breed discrimination between workers and create job ghettos that are difficult to get out of. We generate these difficulties through our funding of both the private and community sectors. Paradoxically, by regularly funding these jobs, we implicitly put their economic and social utility into question. In my opinion, a simpler and more just way of financing unstable jobs, or regions, is to distribute an unconditional income directly to current and potential workers. They would have greater autonomy and we would no longer have to make any arbitrary decisions regarding which industries to subsidize.

Of course we have to help the unemployed get back into the labour market through specifically designed training programs. However, we should eliminate the coercive nature of these programs by no longer tying them to benefit eligibility as we do today. Such a constraint leads to bureaucracy and turns a learning opportunity into a burden. People will find the training programs more credible if they are allowed to take them voluntarily rather than being forced to do so.

Indexing Basic Income to make it more generous

Implementing a BI will allow us to reflect on various aspects of the current welfare state and can help us achieve certain urgent reforms. Nothing, certainly not justice, requires us to maintain the BI at its lowest threshold, and nothing, certainly not justice, compels us to become guardians of the status quo and existing institutions.

We can come up with various ways of making a BI more substantial without necessarily broadening the tax base. First of all, since it constitutes a Basic Income for all citizens, we would naturally have to index it to the cost of living. But we can be a little more daring and suggest that its increase be linked to the annual evolution of the GNP. With low inflation over the last few years, Canada has maintained, on average, a growth rate of between 2 and 4 per cent. This finding contradicts those who still think that growth automatically guarantees a better share of the wealth. Indexing a BI to the evolution of the GNP would allow it to reach substantial levels more quickly, since the GNP is generally higher than the inflation rate. This would certainly be a revolutionary way of thinking with respect to wealth redistribution, but not necessarily an idealistic one. Currently, traditional income security measures do not allow us to follow the evolution in collective wealth since they remain entirely dependent, by definition, on the lowest salaries. A BI, which secures a partial but real decoupling of income and work, allows us to provide a level of redistribution that is as high as possible without conflicting directly with the labour market. It can therefore achieve levels that we could not hope for with certain jobs for which the demand is too low. If the principle of justice at the heart of a BI sets out that everyone can enjoy a share of the collective wealth irrespective of his or her personal contribution to building this wealth, then it would make sense that when the wealth increases, citizens see an increase of the dividends. We could thereby replace a purely assistance-driven rationale with one predicated on equal access to the collective wealth produced by previous and current generations. Of course, things may not always be this simple, and increasing the BI in accordance with the GNP may not always be possible for practical reasons, such as efficiency. However, the burden of proof would be with our governments. This would incidentally be a change for them, since right now, collective wealth is not really a factor when deciding whether or not to increase the level of the social safety net.

Between the cost-of-living adjustment and indexing in accordance with the GNP, there are some intermediary options that are just as viable. It is important to remember that the share of government expenses devoted to the BI should normally decrease as the collective wealth increases. Naturally, the first few years will be crucial and that is why we need to have a successful transition phase. Once this phase is over, however, the BI will be completely integrated with other government expenses, as is the case for education and health care. It should then be able to be indexed in the same way as other social partnership measures.

Replacing student loan and grant programs and re-evaluating social insurance

As the amount of the BI increases, we can start to re-evaluate certain social programs. Student loan and grant programs, for example, should be able to be replaced with a training allowance designed to encourage young people from eighteen to twenty-five to get some training or hold a job that will allow them to develop certain skills. More flexible than current programs but at the same time more restrictive than a totally unconditional BI, this training allowance will help put an end to the academic trap suffered by students who prolong their stay at school because, aside from social assistance, they see it as the only way to finance their immediate needs. This trap seems all the more disheartening considering that many of these students would prefer, at least for a while, to hold a job, work as an intern at a company or take on any other type of activity that would give them some experience. By simplifying educational funding in this way, we make it easier for adults over twenty-five to move from a job to training on a full- or part-time basis. A modern, effective economy should be able to finance people's education at various stages of their lives.

Other social assistance programs could require substantial changes. The most obvious, in my opinion, are the individual or shared insurance programs. These include employment insurance, administered by the federal government but financed through mandatory employer and employee contributions, as well as all pension plans, whether they be group or individual, compulsory or optional. Insurance programs constitute a differed income that is attainable with a decrease in income. Their main attraction is that they spread out the risks, of losing a job, for example. They therefore foster a certain form of social partnership, but only among contributors. As we saw in Chapter 2, income security has been based on these insurance programs for a long time and they seemed to serve their purpose well enough until recent decades. They certainly still have a future, but the introduction of a BI could provide us with the opportunity to revise their role, sometimes significantly.

Insurance programs have a serious flaw: they redistribute relatively little wealth and are satisfied with rolling over a portion of previous income for a limited time. If these revenues were high, the benefits would also be high. By contrast, if the employment earnings were modest and punctuated with periods of inactivity, there would be little or perhaps no benefits at all. As such, insurance mechanisms largely reproduce the inequalities that we find in the labour market. Those with a steady job and a relatively high salary appear to be in the best position to arm themselves against unemployment and to build themselves a gilded pension. At a time such as ours, where qualified people may never have the chance to have a stable job and where salaries are increasingly polarized, the insurance formula proves to be inadequate for many and basically useless for others.

Certain problems are becoming increasingly acute. Let us take the case of employment insurance in Canada. The goal of this program is to better redistribute between workers the risks associated with a temporary loss of employment income. Employment insurance cannot guarantee a subsistence income because the duration of benefits is limited and strictly proportional to the earnings made at the previous job. It is therefore normally aimed at the "involuntarily" unemployed. Various social components, however, were introduced over time (contributions that are independent from job categories, length of benefits adjusted to regional unemployment rates, benefits for parental leaves, and so on). Some of these have undesirable consequences. To demonstrate, I will provide a simple but useful comparison with private insurance plans.

The cost of a private insurance policy normally varies in accordance with the risk represented by the insured. For example, a person with a stable job would contribute much less to employment insurance than someone working in a region where unemployment is high, or another person working in an unstable or seasonal branch of industry. From a strictly economic point of view, the latter two people would, respectively, be encouraged to move or find a job in a more secure industry. Employment insurance has more or less the opposite effect these days, which significantly reduces the mobility of workers between regions and between jobs. People may respond to this by saying that a BI supporter can certainly not be opposed to funding low-income activities. Of course not, but the problem is in the way it is done. Right now, employment insurance puts a portion of the unemployed in a trap similar to that of social assistance. For example, in Canada, there are regions where the economy is overly dependent on employment insurance. This is what happens when entire industries adjust themselves to the eligibility requirements of a particular program. This unemployment trap is not any less harmful than the poverty trap faced by social assistance recipients. It discourages the mobility of these workers and creates long-term dependency. If we succeeded in gradually replacing this type of support with an adequate BI, those holding jobs in the more fragile industries would be doing so more by choice and, above all, completely in the open. For example, we could no longer accuse seasonal workers of being "falsely" involuntarily unemployed and, along with their employers, taking advantage of the system. Furthermore, access to a little more leisure time and a little less work time would be better spread out within the population. This proposal might offend regional supporters, who may see these changes as an end to their economies. This is by no means the objective. We need to have the courage, however, to imagine a world where those who chose to live outside the city can enjoy the same support as those who do not. Only then will they be free of the current employment traps.

So far, I have made no argument for privatizing of employment insurance, an option that I do not see as desirable or even practical. But implementing a BI compels us to clarify the roles of social partnership and insurance within a modern economy and should also free up sums that can be reinvested into a benefit for all. Those who argue for an extension of employment insurance maintain that, in the name of social partnership, it makes sense to transfer benefits from the more advantaged workers to those with less. However, social partnership would be better served if we could redistribute among the general population and not just the workers. The respective roles of insurance and redistribution would therefore be clarified and social partnership would involve everyone. Within the context of increased fiscal competition, it will become crucial that the "assistance" component of these programs be reduced in order to better reflect the positive relationship that normally should exist between tax and benefits. In fact, these social partnership mechanisms among workers are all the more susceptible to downward pressures, since the workers themselves consider them as an effective and affordable means of risk protection. This is one of the forces behind the contribution principle that can explain why, in the opinion of many, it makes sense to maintain the insurance programs, without, however, viewing them as the best tools against poverty and exclusion.[28]

Strengthening the universal pension plan

This confusion between the principles of social insurance and social partnership can also be seen in pension plans. Over the last few years, our governments have encouraged individuals to take charge of their own retirement through generous tax deductions on their pension plans (compulsory or optional, group or individual). This has unfortunately been to the detriment of a basic protection for all. While the popularity of these programs may well be on the rise, they all have the same drawback: reproducing upon retirement the wage inequalities of working life.[29] Current rhetoric on how individuals are accountable for their own retirement has absolutely no meaning for those who are not lucky enough to have a good group pension plan and who do not have enough savings to invest in a private plan. Yet income security for seniors is as important today as it has ever been, as we continue to see a tremendous increase in life expectancy.

What I am about to suggest has a good chance of being unpopular, but we have to take another look at the tax expenditures approved by the government for all individual and group pension plans, particularly because of their regressive nature. We then have to develop a basic pension system for everyone, as a BI would do and as Old Age Security does today, but to a lesser degree since it has been eroded. We need a basic pension that is completely tax-free and that can be drawn concurrently with other annuity income. Those who need more than this Basic Income will still have the luxury of saving and will be motivated to do so simply through interest on their plan rather than through tax reductions that are financed by an increase in everyone's tax rate (in tax matters as well, nothing is free!). The government's job is neither to encourage nor discourage the plan, particularly when the means at their disposal take the form of highly regressive tax shelters.* In the name of justice, defended in the preceding chapter, the government's role in social security is to allow everyone, irrespective of their station in life, to benefit from a Basic Income that is as high as possible to be compatible with economic efficiency and environmental sustainability. Others with greater needs can always have supplements to this basic plan. People's need for additional security does not involve the government, which shouldn't be compelled to spend anything in this area. For the sake of efficiency, however, the government can continue to legislate to provide the framework for or possibly even implement communal pension funds. Those whose needs are not as strong or those with less foresight will then see that social partnership among seniors is based primarily, but not exclusively, on this Basic Income.

---

*This is said of a social policy whose redistributive effects benefit the rich more so than the poor.

Making sure that everyone pays his or her fair share

These changes to the social insurance program, and other changes that are just as influential on the future of a BI, will inevitably lead us to more cohesive mechanisms of social partnership, but these mechanisms will depend on our tax system's ability to tap the collective wealth. BI supporters are often told that simplifying the indirect and direct social assistance programs will have a price: a pronounced taxation of social policies, which inevitably increases the risks and stakes associated with tax evasion. This is a fair comment and we need to use all the means at our disposal to prevent this from happening. Remember, however, that as primary incomes continue to differ, we need to accept an increase in tax rates. For those with nothing to hide, this should not change anything, but those (and there are still many) who evade taxes with impunity will have to learn that they are committing a serious offence within a modern economy that is built on a high degree of reciprocity and cooperation. We are no longer in a feudal society, where poor peasants would risk their lives to hide some of their crop from abusive *seigneurs* in order to feed their families throughout the winter. No one today places their safety or that of their family in danger by paying their taxes. On the contrary, in a well-designed society, a portion of these taxes actually serves to protect citizens from extreme situations. We can therefore understand how everything depends on the way we conceive social partnership and how we incorporate it into the institutional framework. Can a BI respond to the new demands for social partnership? We have to trust that it can, while never hesitating to implement the concrete measures that will get us there.

The future of social partnership

A BI will not suddenly inspire a greater sense of social partnership. However, it could help change the unhealthy practice of targeting policies, which divides the population into categories of taxpayers and debtors. This, in turn, stigmatizes the most disadvantaged and isolates them as a group of petitioners caught up in a power struggle to promote their interests.

Justice has nothing to do with feel-good notions. In general, it strives to formulate political principles that are clear and cohesive and it necessarily relies on institutions that give it substance. When putting themselves before justice, people know that they can count on a certain solidarity that transcends all other forms of social partnership (between spouses, among friends, among members of the same family or the same community and so on) without replacing them entirely. In a society that is consistent with law and justice, this fundamental solidarity inevitably stems from the government, because it alone has the necessary power to correct injustices and behave impartially, using its exclusive coercive power if necessary. But models of social partnership can vary with the times. We sometimes criticize the contemporary welfare state for putting structures in place that favour a cold, institutional and coercive form of social partnership instead of a warm, personalized and voluntary one.[30] In a certain sense, this is true but inevitable for a society that is as developed and pluralistic as ours. This unique (at least from the perspective of more traditional societies) way of establishing social partnership is still the one that suits us the best. It is more effective, less arbitrary and above all, more egalitarian.

Social justice is derived from abstract principles such as equality, impartiality and universality. These principles have shaped political life in the West for two centuries and have led to the emergence of modern democracies. Not everyone, however, is prepared to view their obligations in this way, sometimes because they feel that it is not in their personal interest and sometimes simply because they tend to favour family over strangers. What can proponents of a BI do when confronted with human ego and the tendency of people to feel more partnership with those they know, who resemble them or who share the same skin colour, background, culture or ideas?

The issue stems from difficulties that are real. It would be misleading to say that it is simply a matter of long-term education and that there is nothing we can do about it. The German philosopher Immanuel Kant claimed that justice was possible even for a nation of demons, and we certainly cannot wait around for people to become virtuous to start achieving it. We do, however, need to make sure that these so-called demons understand that their personal interests can be better served by institutions that are just rather than unjust. They also need to know that, over and above their social obligations to fellow citizens, they can always create other social networks that are more tailored to their respective sensibilities.

Reconciling justice with democracy

The first and foremost challenge of social partnership, in our times at least, is to ensure that democracy stands up to our aspirations of justice. There is no preset formula that can make democratic societies into societies that are necessarily just.[31] In truth, democracy and justice are built on tenuous ties that are easy to break. For example, nothing can prevent a well-off majority that is aware of its advantages from disassociating itself from the minority. We have seen this situation many times, and it still exists today. It can generally be explained by the weakness of democratic regimes to respond more quickly to pressure from the most influential groups in society and from people who are well versed on the issues that affect them. In this game, the losers are generally those with the least amount of influence or who have no idea about the issues concerning them, in other words, the poor, the marginalized or those with little education. An obvious example is found in income security policies, which are neglected under government policy. This does nothing to disprove the saying that "services to the poor are poor services." There are many reasons for this. One such reason is that the leaders, and many of those who elect them, are strangers to poverty and exclusion. In this context, it is difficult to make these problems a priority, compared to health care and education, which concern the rich and poor alike. Since people's interests converge when it comes to these areas of social policy, the results of activist-led battles automatically spill over onto society as a whole. In the same way that the poor can expect nothing from a two-tiered health care system, neither must they hope for anything from wealth redistribution formulas that perpetuate the current divide between taxpayers and debtors.

This should serve as a lesson. Instead of waiting for some day in the distant future when people will be compassionate toward the suffering of others, it is more realistic to tackle those institutions that tend to divide people and that, intentionally or unintentionally, encourage differences that undermine social partnership. That is why, when it is possible and justified on the solidarity front, we have to look for universality rather than selectivity, a tax system rather than mutual insurance and finally, a principle of no fees rather than user fees. This is what allows for a BI, which integrates income protection into all of our daily lives, thereby collectivizing it entirely. As well as removing the stigma of recipients, this "forced" social partnership increases potential alliances that foster a better distribution of wealth. How? Simply by ensuring that the most affluent, most educated and therefore most politically influential strata of society are concerned about the existence and financing of this wealth. We therefore end up strengthening social partnership, which benefits primarily those most adversely affected by the power struggle in society.[32] Of course, this strengthening of social partnership is valid for as long as we prefer a BI to the negative income tax, which does not have nearly the same advantages in this area and leads to a two-tiered society. By opting for a BI instead of the negative income tax, we will increase the chance that democracy and justice will be united more often.

Reducing the fiscal sovereignty of governments if necessary

Reconciling democracy with justice is the foremost difficulty facing us as a society today. Another risk concerns the globalization of economies that has tended to accelerate over the last few years. The opening of the markets fundamentally undermines the government's role. I mentioned above that only the government, because it has the legitimate power to enforce, is able to ensure generous forms of redistribution that are well suited to a modern and strong social community. Globalization, however, is turning contemporary governments into true entrepreneurs competing against each other. Governments that take this route are therefore under immense pressure to lower the level of social assistance, to reduce the tax burden on private enterprise, soften taxes of workers who make the highest incomes but who are also among those benefiting from considerable geographic mobility, attract foreign investment by creating tax havens or by funding new enterprises and so on. Unfortunately, none of these would strengthen social partnership.[33] We have governments that are more apt to create free trade zones than to sign social treaties guaranteeing that none of the trade partners will undermine the level of social protection of its citizens. Such treaties should ensure that the wealth generated by the opening of markets compensates those who lose their jobs or whose working conditions deteriorate following changes to the economy. Without agreements of this kind at the international level, a decreasing harmonization is almost inevitable. The ideological leanings of governments do not carry much weight when faced with external pressures. If they do not respond to these pressures, they will be forced out eventually. Social democrats therefore have reasons to worry about this turn of events, even though they have to acknowledge the benefits of an opening of the markets, both here and elsewhere, as well as the impossibility of going back and closing up the borders. So, what can we do for social partnership?

Invoking authority of all kinds does not change anything. We need to define the policies and institutions that are best suited to the new order. Since an increasing number of actions and decisions at the international level have considerable consequences at the national level, we need to see the emergence of international agreements to monitor governments that are equipped with strong social partnership and force others to gradually join them. The opposite will take place if our governments continue to pander to private enterprise.

For all those who feel strongly about social partnership, decreasing the sovereignty of governments in tax matters therefore becomes the mandatory consideration in international economic trade, and we cannot hesitate to demand this if it is imposed in Europe as well as North America. This also holds true for the Canadian federation: if provinces continue to fiscally compete with one another as they have tended to do over the last several years, we will probably have to devise scenarios that would limit their fiscal autonomy so that a Conservative Ontario does not become the norm in terms of social partnership. In these blind, headlong competitive pursuits, good intentions are not enough to get the job done. We need to deal with concrete institutions and try to steer them in our direction.

Strong social partnership but transparent economic relationships

We are sometimes told that one of the main obstacles to a BI will come from our trading partners, particularly the United States, which would see it as a form of disguised business subsidy. Quite honestly, this view does not worry me too much, although we need to establish arguments to counter it. First, the United States themselves "subsidize" low-income jobs in many states. Furthermore, it is impossible to separate what is a subsidy from what is not. Roads that are in good shape, a healthy, educated population, a peaceful social climate: all of these stem in large part from government policies, yet have significant and enviable economic consequences. Contrary to certain preconceived notions, healthy competition does not require that social protection be weak or nonexistent. It demands rather that trade partners adapt to constraints that are similar for everyone.

Contrary to those who predict that a BI will never pass the globalization test, it is a good bet that it will succeed far better than our current tangled web of economic and social policies, ranging from subsidies to multinational corporations to direct support programs for declining sectors. International cooperation will inevitably lead to a simplification and clarification of the rules of the game. We will therefore have to learn to adapt to circumstances. There are two contrasting scenarios to consider. In the first, governments continue to play the role of entrepreneurs, progressively aligning their social protection programs with the smallest common denominator. The winners end up being those with the opportunity to participate in activities that are very strategic or in high demand. In the second scenario, agreements are made between governments to prevent them from competing against each other in the fields of taxation and social policy. We can hope that a BI formula emerges as being the means of social partnership that is best suited to the different countries searching for points of comparison. It is, in fact, a formula that can accept the principle of competition in economic affairs, but which will always reject this same principle when it comes to distributing wealth.

A global Basic Income?

This leads me to one last thought on achieving a form of social partnership that transcends all borders. If, for practical reasons, basic social partnership can only begin where social institutions allow it, in other words at the national level or, in certain cases, below the national level, it should not necessarily stop there. Over the last few years, many European intellectuals have argued for a European BI that would have the advantage of sheltering social solidarity frameworks from competition with member countries and achieving the first step toward a more cosmopolitan form of social partnership.[34] Others, including two Nobel Laureates, have even argued for a global BI.[35] I will not try and give an opinion as to the short-term feasibility of these projects. I do, however, feel that such expansions of the BI are not only desirable but also necessary. They remind us of how interdependent we are and that not everyone benefits to the same degree from a global division of work and resources. Deep down, I believe that we will have to reach this level of BI eventually, even if, for practical purposes, we have to start by restricting ourselves to the institutions that allow it, before following up with a broadening of social partnership. Over time, people learn that what divides them is very little compared to what unites them: a vast collective wealth that they are responsible for managing, not only for themselves, but also for future generations.

A BI will never be achieved overnight. This is not such a bad thing, since we will have time to prepare and reflect on its many consequences. We must never forget that the spirit of social partnership that fuels a BI is already evident in certain institutional achievements that we can be proud of: free education and universal access to health care. We need to continue in this direction, while focusing now on the idea of "economic citizenship."

Having finished this chapter, readers will realize there are many steps we can take right now toward achieving the dream of a BI. Starting immediately, we need to take up the gauntlet to maintain and reinforce the universal programs that we have in place today. We also need to find ways to decrease the importance of tax programs that benefit the most affluent in society. Once we have taken these steps, it will become increasingly important to define transparent forms of distribution. At that point, a proposal such as the one defended in these pages could truly capture the imagination of the nation. This does not mean waiting passively for some sort of revolution in thinking but rather coming up with sound structural changes that are inspired by the same clear vision of what is worthwhile. Some may find that this is not enough. I invite them to help me to do more, by drawing on the principles that guide a BI and by motivating those around them.

Conclusion

Goodwill and pious hopes are not enough to reform society. We also need a clear vision of the concrete steps to be taken. I have tried to communicate this research according to the "Archimedian point," which allows us to think about institutions that are better suited to new contexts and our aspirations for justice. There is still a lot of room for further study by those who would like to pursue their own research on a BI and its principles.

I would also like to remind readers that the numerous technical aspects that I have raised, particularly in the last chapter, should never monopolize future debate. All these considerations on taxation, benefit recovery rates and the effects of redistribution are certainly important, and the work of experts should allow us to see these issues more clearly. However, beyond this research and the many heated controversies that will occupy us over the next few years, what we need more than anything is for each of us to understand the urgency of determining the type of social partnership that is best suited to our times. We have to take an unbiased approach, using the best empirical information available, while disregarding the many artificial political divides that we could otherwise be drawn into. A BI certainly brings new perspectives to the relationships that citizens must develop within a just society. It is from this new world, which has already partially been built, that we must lead the debate.

The welfare state is at a crossroads. As its inevitable transformations begin to unfold, we have to do everything in our power not to unconsciously or irrecoverably cast aside our greatest successes to date.

Sainte-Foy, October 20, 2000

Appendix A

Comparison between the distributive structures of the negative income tax and a BI.

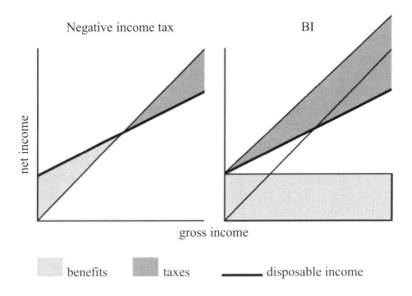

Note: These diagrams clearly show that the negative income tax results in fewer government expenditures than the BI (compare the pale grey areas). The tax needed to finance these two measures is consequently much more significant in the second diagram (compare the dark grey areas). However, in terms of taxpayer costs, the two solutions are strictly identical and each citizen's disposable income remains the same. This result, described by some as "counterintuitive," can be explained by a simple "income effect" (net income after taxes and benefits). With a BI, everyone will receive more direct benefits from the government, but it is understood that they will be taxed more on their gross income.

Appendix B

Web sites devoted primarily to Basic Income

Association pour l'instauration d'un revenu d'existence (AIRE)
Country: France
AIRE promotes BI in France. This site describes the project, as well as actions AIRE has taken over the past two years to promote it.

Address: http://perso.wanadoo.fr/mjsi/

Basic Income European Network (BIEN)
Region: Europe
This is likely the most important and most comprehensive site dedicated to a BI. BIEN's goal is to serve as a link between partisan individuals and groups or simply those who are interested in a BI and to encourage informed discussions on the topic. The site contains extensive documentation through their quarterly newsletter (available on the site), a large annotated bibliography (in many languages), texts presented to the legislature, Internet links, etc.

Address: http://www.basicincome.org

Basic Income/Canada
Country: Canada
Basic Income/Canada (BI/Canada) maintains a Web site and an e-mail discussion group. Their coordinator is Sally Lerner. To be included on the BI/Canada e-mail list to receive periodic newsletters, contact: lerner@watser1.uwaterloo.ca. BI/Canada's Web site (maintained by Tim Rourke) features essays and commentary on Basic Income in a Canadian context.

Address: http://www.ourlives.ca/bitrunk.html

Also affiliated with BI/Canada is Futurework, an international e-mail forum on how to deal with the new realities created by economic globalization and technological change.

Address: http://www.fes.uwaterloo.ca/Research/FW

Citizen's Income Study Centre
Country: England
This group was founded in 1984 under the name of Basic Income Research Group and is dedicated to the study of all aspects of reform pertaining to a "citizen's income."

Address: http://www.ownbase.org.uk/citizens-income/index.html

The Future Work
Country: Canada
This site is a discussion forum on new job realities, technological changes and globalization. It is relatively new but puts the spotlight on a BI in the Canadian context.

Address: http://www.fes.uwaterloo.ca/Research/FW/

Organisation Advocating Support Income in Australia (OASIS)
Country: Australia
This site contains a series of texts and newsletters promoting a BI and covering other related topics.

Address: http://www.satcom.net.au/supportincome

Universal Basic Income New Zealand (UBINZ)
Country: New Zealand
This site has a heading devoted to the history of a BI and includes a series of documents, some of which were presented at national conferences, as well as links to other related sites.

Address: http://www.geocities.com/~ubinz/

Vereniging Basisinkomen
Country: Netherlands
This site belongs to the *Vereniging Basisinkomen* (Basic Income Association) which was created in 1991 with the goal of coordinating research and ways of implementing a BI in the Netherlands. Their quarterly newsletters are available on this site.

Address: http://www.wxs.nl/~schafer

Citizenship, Income and Society Webring
This is a search engine that allows people to find sites and information on BI.

Address: http://www.citizensincome.org/ring/ring.shtml

Glossary

Workers
Economists use this term to designate people who participate in the labour market and have salaried jobs.

Non-workers
Economists use this term to designate people who, as opposed to the working poor, do not have any employment earnings.

Marginal tax rate
The marginal tax rate equals the tax rate for all secondary income. For economists, it constitutes a significant variable in measuring an individual's work incentive. The "effective" (or implicit) rate is a way of considering the tax treatment of certain benefits.

Regressive
This is said of a social policy whose redistributive effects benefit the rich more so than the poor.

Workfare
Derived from the word "welfare," this term is used somewhat pejoratively to designate income support measures that are strictly conditional upon some form of work.

Endnotes

CHAPTER 1 • Waging War Against Poverty Instead of the Poor

1. Certain historic landmarks are recalled in the following works: Tony Fitzpatrick, *Freedom and Security: An Introduction to the Basic Income Debate* (London: Macmillan Press, 1999); Tony Walter, *Basic Income: Freedom from Poverty, Freedom to Work* (London and New York: Marion Boyar, 1989); Walter Van Trier, *Every One A King*, doctorate dissertation (Louvain Catholic University: Sociology Department, 1995); Philippe Van Parijs, "La préhistoire du débat: l'ombre de Speenhamland," *La Revue nouvelle* 4 (1985): 395–399. With respect to Canada, there is some interesting reading in Appendix 1 of the research conducted by Human Resources Development Canada, *The Guaranteed Annual Income: an information paper* (Ottawa: 1994).
2. Among these utopian and visionary thinkers are Thomas Paine (1737–1809), Charles Fourier (1772–1837), Edward Bellamy (1850–1898) and Bertrand Russell (1872–1970).
3. What comes particularly to mind are the important debates that influenced American political life during these years. Reputable economists including R. Theobald, M. Harrington, R. Heilbroner, G. Myrdal, J. K. Galbraith and P. Samuelson argued for a guaranteed minimum income. Influential politicians were also quite interested in the idea. This period and the events that unfortunately led to the failed legislative attempt in this area are raised in Daniel Moynihan, *The Politics of a Guaranteed Income: The Nixon Administration and the Family Assistance Plan* (New York: Random House, 1973). French readers will find a brief summary in Mark Rogin Anspach, "L'archipel du Welfare américain. Âge d'abondance, Âge de pierre," in *La Revue du MAUSS*, vol. 7, no. 1 (1996): 37–82.
4. Jan Tinbergen (1969), James Meade (1977), Herbert Simon (1978) and James Tobin (1981).

5. Many BI supporters are grouped under the banner of the Basic Income European Network (BIEN). This international association unites researchers and activists wanting to study and promote a BI. BIEN has a Web site that is regularly updated: (http://www.basicincome.org). The site includes a large annotated biliography.
6. For an overview of various BI justifications, see Philippe Van Parijs, ed., *Arguing for Basic Income* (London and New York: Verso, 1992); Claudine Leleux, *Travail ou revenu? Pour un revenu inconditionnel* (Paris: Cerf, 1998). *La Revue du MAUSS* published a special issue in 1996 on the topic: *Vers un revenu minimum inconditionnel?* vol. 7, no 1.This work includes contributions of both supporters and opponents. For Canada: Sally Lerner, Charles Clark and Robert Needham, *Basic Income: Economic Security for All Canadians* (Toronto: Between the Lines, 1999).
7. In Europe, environmentalists were the first to be interested in this proposal. Today, liberals and socialists are not to be outdone. For a good overview of the different motivations of these great political families, see Tony Fitzpatrick, *Freedom and Security: An Introduction to the Basic Income Debate* (London: Macmillan Press, 1999). For an update on political debates in Europe, read: Robert Van der Veen and Loek Groot, eds., *Basic Income on the Agenda: Policy Options and Political Feasibility* (Amsterdam: Amsterdam University Press, 2000).
8. For Thomas Paine, see his speech on agrarian justice presented to the French National Assembly in 1796, in which this philosopher of fundamental rights argues that every French citizen who has reached the age of twenty-one should receive compensation for the private appropriation of land, which, in his eyes, inevitably consitutes an injustice for future generations. See Thomas Paine, "Agrarian Justice" in P.F. Foner, ed., *The Life and Major Writings of Thomas Paine* (New Jersey: Citadel Press, 1974), 605–23. For Charles Fourier, read his great work dating from 1836: *La Fausse Industrie, morcelée, répugnante, mensongère, et l'antidote, l'industrie naturelle, combinée, attrayante, véridique, donnant quadruple produit et perfection extrême en toutes qualités* (Paris: Anthropos, 1967). Fourier argued for minimum assistance for have-nots (in kind rather than in cash) to compensate for their difficulty in meeting their needs in societies where natural laws of fishing, hunting and gathering are necessarily restricted by civilization and private property. One of his disciples, Belgian lawyer Joseph Charlier, advanced the first proposal for a strictly conditional dividend

allocated regularly from the time of birth. See *La Question sociale résolue. Précédée du testament philosophique d'un penseur* (Brussels: P. Weissenbruch, 1894).

9. See Clifford H. Douglas, *Economic Democracy* (Sudbury: Bloomfield, 1974 [1920]) and *Social Credit* (London: Spottiswoode, 1934). Remember that in England, this proposal was preceded by that of Dennis Milner, *Higher Production by a Bonus on National Output: A Proposal for a Minimum Income for All Varying with National Productivity* (London: George Allen & Unwin, 1920). Its main goal was to help in the reconstruction after the First World War. Milner's proposal is sometimes considered to be the first modern BI proposal. See Walter Van Trier, *Every One A King*, doctoral dissertation (Louvain Catholic University, Sociology Department: 1995).

10. Source: Statistics Canada, www.Statcan.ca/francais/Pgdb/People/Families/famil41a_f.htm

11. See Thomas Piketty, *L'économie des inégalités* (Paris: La Découverte, 1997).

12. On the history of the welfare state in Canada and Quebec, I refer to two works in particular: Dennis Guest, *The Emergence of Social Security in Canada* (Vancouver: University of British Columbia Press, 1997) and Yves Vaillancourt, *L'évolution des politiques sociales au Canada et au Québec, 1940–1960* (Montréal: Presses de l'Université de Montréal, 1988). For a more theoretical perspective: Erik Oddvar Eriksen and Jørn Loftager, eds., *The Rationality of the Welfare State* (Oslo: Scandinavian University Press, 1996).

13. These figures were obtained simply by comparing the average Canadian minimum wage and the low-income cut-offs established by Statistics Canada for people living in centres with more than 500,000 people.

14. These figures were taken from the National Council of Welfare, *Poverty Profile 1995* (Ottawa: Ministry of Supply and Services, 1997).

15. For a more detailed account of the poverty trap's multiple effects, see Philippe Van Parijs, "De la trappe au socle, l'allocation universelle contre le chômage," *La Revue du MAUSS* 7 (1996): 90–104.

16. Bernard Fortin, Guy Lacroix and Jean-Yves Duclos, *L'univers de l'aide sociale: les plus démunis peuvent-ils s'en sortir?* (Recherche sociale, Conseil québécois de la recherche sociale) vol. 6, no. 1 (1999).

17. See Robert Theobald, ed., *The Guaranteed Income* (New York: Doubleday, 1966).

18. For further reading see Theresa Funiciello, *Tyranny of Kindness: Dismantling the Welfare System to End Poverty in America* (New York: Atlantic Monthly Press, 1993). For a more detailed analysis of various American experiences, try David T. Ellwood, *Poor Support: Poverty in the American Family* (New York: Basic Books, 1988).
19. On this topic, read Karl Polanyi, *The Great Transformation: The Political and Economic Origins of Our Time* (Boston: Beacon Press, 1957 [1944c]).
20. There are other advantages in providing a BI unconditionally. I present these in Chapter 2 in the sections entitled "Economic grounds for a Basic Income" and "A Basic Income and social justice."
21. Thinking of a BI in terms of integrating it with taxation is fundamental to understanding its progressive nature. The income-effect distinguishes improvements in gross income from improvements in net income. It is true that a BI will increase the gross income of every citizen but only the after-tax income of the most disadvantaged in society. This progressiveness, however, does not come about automatically, and that is why the transition period leading up to a BI is so important, as I indicate in Chapter 3 in the section entitled "Short-term implementation scenario." For further reading on this topic, see Hermione Parker, *Instead of the Dole: An Enquiry into Integration of the Tax and Benefit Systems* (London: Routledge, 1989).

Chapter 2 • Reconciling Efficiency and Fairness in a Changing World

1. On the relationship between efficiency and fairness, see the classic text by Arthur M. Okun, *Equality and Efficiency: The Big Tradeoff* (Washington: The Brookings Institution, 1975). In French, read the excellent work by Marc Fleurbaey, *Théories économiques de la justice* (Paris: Economica, 1996).
2. See Vilfrero Pareto, *Cours d'économie politique* (Geneva: Droz, 1964).
3. The reader simply has to understand that, in terms of economic choice, nothing is perfectly static, and that agents are continually adapting to new constraints.
4. On this theme and many others relating to social justice, I owe a lot to John Rawls, *A Theory of Justice* (Cambridge: Belknap Press of Harvard University, 1971).
5. See Amartya Sen, *Inequality Reexamined* (New York/Cambridge:

Russell Sage Foundation/Harvard University Press, 1992).
6. On this point, I share the same point of view as John Rawls in *A Theory of Justice* (Cambridge: Belknap Press of Harvard University, 1971) (see particularly sections 11 to 13).
7. In this section, I have greatly benefited from Nicholas Barr's excellent work, *The Economics of the Welfare State* (Stanford: Stanford University Press, 1993).
8. We have to add to this list the other forms of social insurance (unemployment, old age, disability) which, on a strictly private basis, would never provide adequate coverage for the population as a whole.
9. See Jean Baechler, *Le Capitalisme* (Paris: Gallimard, 1995).
10. Beveridge's model will therefore take precedence over the proposals of another English reformer, an important figure in BI history, Lady Juliet Rhys-Williams. As opposed to Beveridge, she proposed that a dividend be paid out that would replace previous unemployment allowances and other forms of poverty relief. See *Something to Look Forward To* (London: Macdonald, 1943).
11. See Jeremy Rifkin, *The End of Work* (New York: G.B. Putnam's Sons, 1994).
12. See Organization for Economic Co-operation and Development (OECD), *Making work pay: taxation, benefits, employment and underemployment* (Paris: 1997). This document offers an excellent overview of the global changes affecting the job market and compares national income- and employment-support strategies.
13. These generalities are well known. For a more detailed account, try Claus Offe, "Droits et ressources économiques du citoyen: vers un nouvel équilibre?" in Organization de coopération et de développement économique (OCDE), *Cohésion sociale et mondialisation de l'économie* (Paris: 1997), 91–121. Also see Adrian Wood, *North-South Trade, Employment and Inequality* (Oxford: Oxford University Press, 1994).
14. It is worth remembering that four Nobel Laureates in economics support the proposal (see note four in Chapter 1). Also, I would like to quote the assistant editor of the *Financial Times*, Samuel Brittan, and world-renowned economist Anthony B. Atkinson. For Brittan, read *Capitalism with a Human Face* (Aldershot: Edward Elgar, 1995) and *Beyond the Welfare State: An Examination of Basic Income in a Market Economy* (London: Aberdeen University Press, 1990) (in collaboration with Steven Webb). For Atkinson, read *Public Economics in Action: The Basic Income/Flat Tax* (Oxford: Oxford

University Press, 1995). Also read James Meade, *Full Employment Regained?: An Agathopian Dream* (Cambridge: Cambridge University Press, 1995) and Guy Standing, "Meshing Labour Flexibility with Security: an Answer to Mass Unemployment" in *International Labour Review* 125 (1986): 87–106. In Quebec, businessmen Charles Sirois and Robert Dutil offered a defense that was partially, but not exclusively, based on economics. Read Charles Sirois, *Passage obligé. Passeport pour l'ère nouvelle* (Montreal: Les éditions de l'Homme, 1999) and Robert Dutil, *La Juste Inégalité. Essai sur la liberté, l'égalité et la démocratie* (Montreal: Québec/Amérique, 1995).

15. Objections to a BI from the Left can sometimes be quite extreme: "pure liberal utopianism"; "hell paved with good intentions"; "utopia at cross-purposes"; "submission to the capitalist order," and so on. In France, fortunately, these visceral reactions have calmed down a little, primarily because of the support of Leftist philosopher André Gorz. See his lastest work, *Misères du présent, richesse du possible* (Paris: Galilée, 1997). Not so long ago, Gorz himself was not terribly convinced by the proposal. In particular, see *Métamorphoses du travail. Quête du sens et critique de la raison économique* (Paris: Galilée, 1988).

16. This tendency to associate economic arguments strictly with the Right is examined in Tony Fitzpatrick's excellent work, *Freedom and Security: an Introduction to the Basic Income Debate* (London: Macmillan Press, 1999).

17. See the Government of Quebec, Department of Finance, *Les Taux marginaux implicites de taxation* (Quebec: 1999). For international comparisons, Organization for Economic Co-operation and Development (OECD), *Making work pay: taxation, benefits, employment and unemployment* (Washington: 1997) (particularly Chapter 4).

18. I will come back to the costs of a BI in Chapter 3. For further details, read Timothy Besley, "Means Testing versus Universal Provision in Poverty Alleviation" in *Economica* 57 (1990): 119–129.

19. See Anthony B. Atkinson's recent arguments supporting universal mechanisms in *Poverty in Europe* (London: Blackwell, 1998).

20. This type of argument directly corresponds to the words of one of our great thinkers on the welfare state, Richard Titmuss. On this topic, read "Universal and Selective Social Services" in Brian Abel-Smith and Kay Titmuss, eds., *The Philosophy of Welfare: Selected Writings of Richard M. Titmuss* (London: Allen & Unwin [1987]), 128–140.

Also read Robert E. Goodin, "Towards a Minimally Presumptuous Social Welfare Policy" in Philippe Van Parijs, ed., *Arguing for Basic Income* (London: Verso, 1992), 195–214; and also Robert E. Goodin, *Reasons for Welfare* (Princeton: Princeton University Press, 1988).

21. This argument has been particularly well developed in Jean-Marc Ferry's work, *L'Allocation universelle. Pour un revenu de citoyenneté* (Paris: Cerf, 1995). See also Yoland Bresson, *Le Partage du temps et des revenus* (Paris: Economica, 1994).
22. See Jeremy Rifkin, *The End of Work* (New York: G.B. Putnam's Sons, 1994).
23. See Philippe Van Parijs, "De la trappe au socle, l'allocation universelle contre le chômage," *La Revue du MAUSS* 7 (1996): 90–104.
24. See Guy Standing, *Global Labour Flexibility: Seeking Distributive Justice* (Basingstoke: Macmillan, 1999).
25. It seems logical to want to fight against this employment situation, but most of the time it involves economic decisions that are beyond our immediate political control. Furthermore, closing borders or limiting the use of technological power in order to preserve traditional jobs would be economically harmful and probably morally selfish with respect to developing countries that stand to gain from an increased mobility of capital and knowledge. On this topic, read the excellent work by Pierre-Noël Giraud, *L'inégalité du monde. Économie du monde contemporain* (Paris: Gallimard, 1996).
26. See James Meade, *Full Employment Regained?: An Agathopian Dream* (Cambridge: Cambridge University Press, 1995). For another perspective on government funding of certain jobs, see Edmund S. Phelps, *Rewarding Work: How to Restore Participation and Self-Support to Free Entreprise* (Cambridge: Harvard University Press, 1997).
27. Samuel Brittan, *Capitalism with a Human Face* (Aldershot: Edward Elgar, 1995); James Meade, *Full Employment Regained?: An Agathopian Dream* (Cambridge: Cambridge University Press, 1995).
28. See article seven of the International Covenant of Economic, Social and Cultural Rights, which recognizes the right of every person to an "equitable wage."
29. Milton Friedman, who never defended the principle of a BI but rather a competing proposal called "the negative tax" (refer to the section entitled "Various funding options to explore" in Chapter 3) supported such a dismantling of social measures in "The Case for the Negative Income Tax: a View from the Right" in J. H. Bunzel, ed., *Issues of*

American Public Policy (Englewood Cliffs: Prentice Hall, 1968 [1966]), 111–120. For a Leftist version, see also the appeal launched beginning in 1984 by the Collectif Charles Fourier in Belgium: "Eliminate unemployment benefits, legal pensions, minimex, family allowances, tax abatements and credits for dependents, academic scholarships, special temporary relief structures, third work circuits, government assistance to struggling companies. But provide each citizen with enough money every month to cover the basic needs of an individual living alone.... At the same time, deregulate the labour market. Abolish any legislation that imposes a minimum wage or a maximum work period. Get rid of all administrative obstacles to part-time work. Reduce the age at which mandatory schooling ends. Eliminate the requirement to take retirement at a determined age. Do all of this, and then observe what happens. Pay particular attention to the effect on work, its content and the technologies and human relationships that it encompasses." (trans.) This text appeared in *La Revue nouvelle*, vol. 81, no. 1 (April 1985): 345–360. Most of the signatories have since changed their mind on this radical way of introducing a BI.
30. See James Meade, *Full Employment Regained?: An Agathopian Dream* (Cambridge: Cambridge University Press, 1995).
31. This objection inevitably leads back to the small town of Speenhamland at the end of the eighteenth century. Karl Polanyi describes this in *The Great Transformation: The Political and Economic Origins of Our Time* (Boston: Beacon Press, 1957 [1944c]).
32. See André Gorz, *Misères du présent. Richesse du possible* (Paris: Galilée, 1997).
33. Pierre Rosanvallon, *La Crise de l'état-providence* (Paris: éditions du Seuil, 1981); Carl Wellman, *Welfare Right* (Totowa: Rowman and Littlefield, 1982); Erik Oddvar Eriksen and Jørn Loftager, eds., *The Rationality of the Welfare State* (Oslo: Scandinavian University Press, 1996).
34. I owe a lot to Philippe Van Parijs, *Real Freedom for All* (Oxford: Clarendon Press, 1995). In French, read *Sauver la solidarité* (Paris: Cerf, 1995) and *Refonder la solidarité* (Paris: Cerf, 1997).
35. We need to understand the source of the misgivings of two such different philosophers, André Gorz and John Rawls. For Gorz, read *Métamorphoses du travail. Quête du sens. Critique de la raison économique* (Paris: Galilée, 1988). In his latest work, however, his opinion has changed and he completely supports the proposal's

unconditionality. See *Misères du présent. Richesse du possible* (Paris: Galilée, 1997). As for Rawls, many authors have looked to associate his concept of justice with the BI principle. This particularly applies to Philippe Van Parijs (see *Refonder la solidarité* [Paris: Cerf, 1996]), Samuel Brittan (see *Capitalism with a Human Face* [Aldershot: Edward Elgard, 1995]) and Robert Dutil (see *La Juste Inégalité. Essai sur la liberté, l'égalité et la démocratie* [Montreal: Québec/Amérique, 1995]). It is, however, clear that Rawls' theory concentrates too much on reciprocity (society as an equitable system of cooperation) to support such a measure: "So those who surf all day off Malibu must find a way to support themselves and would not be entitled to public funds." See *Political Liberalism* (New York: Columbia University Press, 1993) 182n. For more on this common resistance to a BI, read Stuart White, "Liberal equality, exploitation and the case for an unconditional basic income" in *Political Studies* 45 (1997): 312–326. Also read François Blais "Loisir, travail et réciprocité: une justification rawlsienne de l'allocation universelle est-elle possible?" in *Loisir et société/Society and Leisure*, vol. 22, no 2 (1999): 337–353.

36. See Mark Rogin Anspach, "L'archipel du Welfare américain. Âge d'abondance, âge de pierre" in *La Revue du MAUSS*, vol. 7, no. 1 (1996): 37–82. Also see Jean-Claude Barbier and Jerôme Gautié, eds., *Les Politiques de l'emploi en Europe et aux États-Unis* (Paris: Presses universitaires de France, 1998).

37. Furthermore, this does not exclude a consensus regarding certain public values (tolerance, equality, each person's right to lead the life he or she chooses and so on). For more on this topic, see *Libéralisme Politique* (Paris: Presses universitaires de France, 1995 [1993c]), and Charles Larmore, *Modernité et morale* (Paris: Presses universitaires de France,1993.)

38. For a contemporary defense of justice as a mutual benefit, read David Gauthier, *Morals by Agreement* (Oxford: Clarendon Press, 1986). Brian Barry does an excellent critique in *Theories of Justice* (Berkeley: University of California Press, 1989).

39. See Jon Elster's comment on this topic in "Comment on Van der Veen and Van Parijs" in *Theory and Society*, vol. 15, no 15 (1986): 709–721.

40. For a criticism of the meritocratic concept of justice: *Political Liberalism* (New York: Columbia University Press, 1993) 182.

41. This point of view is entirely set apart from more communitarian concepts of justice. See André Berten, Pablo Da Silveira and Hervé

Pourtois, *Libéraux et communautariens* (Paris: Presses universitaires de France, 1997).
42. See Hillel Steiner's "Three Just Taxes" in Philippe Van Parijs, ed., *Arguing for Basic Income* (London and New York: Verso, 1992).
43. This well-known theme in political philosophy is admirably developed by Hillel Steiner, *An Essay on Rights* (Oxford: Blackwell, 1994).
44. This perspective may seem revolutionary to some readers. In fact, it was defended by a majority of liberal thinkers such as Locke, Rousseau and Kant who, each in their own way, foresaw insurmountable difficulties in completely appropriating rare resources. For a contemporary analysis, see Ronald Dworkin, "What is Equality? Part II: Equality of Resources" in *Philosophy and Public Affairs* 10 (1981): 283–345 and also Philippe Van Parijs, *Real Freedom for All* (Oxford: Clarendon Press, 1995).
45. For a brilliant contemporary justification for providing an allotment to each young American once they reach adulthood, read Bruce Ackerman and Anne Alstott, *The Stakeholder Society* (New Haven: Yale University Press, 1999).
46. For a more in-depth examination of this issue, see Philippe Van Parijs, *Real Freedom for All* (Oxford: Clarendon Press, 1995).
47. See Ronald Dworkin, *Taking Rights Seriously* (London: Duckworth, 1977).
48. Some of the most tenacious objections to a BI are in this same vein. I think particularly of Pierre Rosanvallon, *La Nouvelle Question sociale. Repenser l'État-providence* (Paris: Seuil, 1995) and Robert Castel, *Les Métamorphoses de la question sociale. Une chronique du salariat* (Paris: Éditions de l'Atelier, 1997). Both accuse the proposal of promoting a split society.
49. See Dominique Méda, "L'ambiguïté d'un revenu minimum inconditionnel" in *La Revue du MAUSS*, vol. 7, no. 1 (1996): 169–173. These concerns are also present in Pierre Rosanvallon's brief remarks on the subject in *La Nouvelle Question sociale* (Paris: Seuil, 1995), 122–125.
50. Claus Offe claims, for these reasons, that the "right to work" and the "right to compete for work" are irreconcilable. See "Full Employment: Asking the Wrong Question" in Eriksen and Jørn Loftager, eds., *The Rationality of the Welfare State* (Oslo: Scandinavian University Press, 1996), 121–133.
51. See Jon Elster, "Is there (or should there be) a right to work?" in Amy Gutmann, ed., *Democracy and the Welfare State* (Princeton:

Princeton University Press, 1988), 53–78.
52. For more on this topic, read Dominique Méda, *Le Travail: une valeur en voie de disparition* (Paris: Aubier, 1995).
53. The idea that a BI can be justified by accumulating capital and technology that have been passed down to us was fundamental to "utopian" authors such as Paine, Fourier and Edward Bellamy. See Bellamy's work *Looking Backward* (Harmondsworth: Penguin Books, 1983 [1897]) and *Equality* (New York: Appleton, 1897).
54. This distinction among economic, social and individual values is important in ethical arguments supporting a BI.
55. I completely agree here with Jean-Marc Ferry's arguments for developing a "quaternary" sector comprising self-directed personal activities that are entirely removed from the dictates of the market and automation. See Jean-Marc Ferry, *L'Allocation universelle. Pour un revenu de citoyenneté* (Paris: Cerf, 1995).
56. Partisans of socialism must understand that no socio-economic system, including all forms of socialism, is able to guarantee total fairness when it comes to redistributing wealth in favour of the most disadvantaged. That is why wealth redistribution will always be a necessary and determining factor in a society that aspires to treat all its citizens equally. I would even say that, in its own way, a BI can nicely recapture some of the great ideals of socialism, such as the principles of "freedom from paid employment" or the leitmotif "to everyone according to their needs." For more on this subject, see Robert J. Van der Veen and Philippe Van Parijs, "A Capitalist Road to Communism" in *Theory and Society*, vol. 15, no. 5 (1986): 635–656.
57. Formulated for the first time by John Rawls before being taken up again and discussed by a host of philosophers and economists, "maximin" (maximizing the situation of the have-nots) has been and continues to be popular in economic justice literature. For an analysis see Marc Fleurbaey, *Théories économiques de la justice* (Paris: Economica, 1996).
58. On the principle of maintaining productive capacity for future generations, see Brian Barry, "Intergenerational Justice in Energy Policy," in Douglas Maclean and Peter G. Brown, eds., *Energy and the Future* (Totowa: Rowman and Littlefield, 1983), 15–30 and Philippe Van Parijs, "Du patrimoine naturel aux régimes de retraite" in *Refonder la solidarité* (Paris: Cerf, 1997), 67–95.
59. I completely agree with the criticism of the current welfare state made by John Rawls. See the related passage in the introduction of the new

English edition of *A Theory of Justice*, which appeared in 1999.

Chapter 3 • Implementing a Basic Income Starting Now

1. To get an idea of this, consult the "news" section of the Basic Income European Network Web site (see Appendix B). In Canada, the latest figures have come from Sally Lerner, Charles Clark and Robert Needham, *Basic Income: Economic Security for All Canadians* (Toronto: Between the Lines, 1999). In France, a debate on a negative tax was outstandingly begun by Roger Godino "Pour la création d'une allocation compensatrice de revenu" in *Pour une réforme du RMI* (Paris: notes from the Fondation Saint-Simon, 1999). For England, see Bill Jordan, Phil Agulnik, Duncan Burbidge and Stuart Duffin, *Stumbling Towards Basic Income* (London: Citizen's Income Study Centre, 2000). For Belgium, read Bruno Gilain and Philippe Van Parijs, "L'allocation universelle: Un scénario de court terme et son impact distributif," *Revue belge de sécurité sociale* (first quarter 1996): 5–74. For Ireland: Brigid Reynolds and Sean Healy, *Towards an Adequate Income for All* (Conference of Religious of Ireland, 1994).
2. Royal Commission on the Economic Union and Development Prospects for Canada, *Report* (Ottawa: Ministry of Supply and Services, 1985) (Take a particular look at pages 794–802).
3. See page 783 of the report.
4. Read, for example, Duncan Cameron, "La commission Macdonald et l'autte rapport Macdonald," *Perception*, vol. 9, no. 1 (1985): 10–12 as well as Paul R. Bélanger and Benoît Lévesque, "Le rapport Macdonald et le marché du travail" in *Perception*, vol. 9, no. 3 (1986): 17–19.
5. Commission of Inquiry on Unemployment Insurance, *Report* (Ottawa: Ministry of Supply and Services, 1986).
6. For further reading, see Hermione Parker, *Instead of the Dole: An Enquiry into Integration of the Tax and Benefit Systems* (London: Routledge, 1989) and by the same author: *Taxes, Benefit and Family Life: The Seven Deadly Traps* (London: Institute of Economic Affairs, 1995).
7. This assessment will be useful in examining concrete implementation scenarios.
8. Michel Bernard, Michel Chartrand and Jean-Marc Ferry rely heavily on this factor in justifying a full, rather than partial, BI. For Bernard and Chartrand, see *Manifeste pour un revenu de citoyenneté* (Montreal: Éditions du renouveau québécois, 1999). For Ferry, see

L'Allocation universelle. Pour un revenu de citoyenneté (Paris: Cerf, 1995).

9. On these difficulties, see Anthony B. Atkinson in *Public Economics in Action:. The Basic Income/Flat Tax* (Oxford: Oxford University Press, 1995).

10. For more on the consequences of a BI for women, read the excellent work by Ingrid Robeyns: "An Emancipation Fee or Hush Money? The advantages and disadvantages of a basic income for women's emancipation and well-being," presented at the 7th International Convention of the Basic Income European Network, Amsterdam. The main conclusions emphasized that the impact of a BI on women varies highly according to wage category and socio-professional group. Also see Hermione Parker, *Citizen's Income and Women*, Basic Income Research Group Discussion Paper no. 2 (London: Citizen's Income Study Centre, 1993).

11. See Roger Godino "Réformer la fiscalité des revenus faibles en créant une Allocation Compensatrice de Revenu" in *La Lettre* (*Action pour le Renouveau Socialiste*) 84 (Paris, 2000).

12. The negative tax was sounded out for the first time by American George Stigler in "The Economics of Minimum Wage Legislation," *American Economic Review* (1946): 358–365. The economist preferred this solution to a universal minimum wage. Friedman took up this idea in his famous 1962 work, *Capitalism and Freedom* (Chicago: University of Chicago Press, 1975 [1960]). He then developed it in "The Case for the Negative Income Tax: a View from the Right," *Issues of American Public Policy*, edited by J.H. Bunzel (Englewood Cliffs: Prentice Hall, 1968), 111–120. From Friedman's perspective, the negative tax was going to allow us to deflate the bureaucratic welfare state and free the labour market from certain wage and social constraints. Also read Robert Theobald, *Free Men and Free Markets* (New York: Anchor Books, 1965). In French, also refer to the work by Lionel Stoleru, *Vaincre la pauvreté dans les pays riches* (Paris: Flammarion, 1974).

13. In Quebec, this takes the form of the APPORT program.

14. "… the work decisions of benefit recipients are also influenced by the way benefits are administered and the penalties this imposes (sometimes inadvertently) on those considering re-entering the labour force. Where administrative procedures are cumbersome and time consuming, or where the rules themselves discourage benefit reapplication (for example, by imposing waiting periods), the perceived risks of accepting a job can offset any potential gain in

income...." This quote is taken from *Fiscal Studies*, vol. 16, no. 2 (1995): 58.

15. At the same time as Friedman and in the wake of guaranteed minimum income debates in the United States, James Tobin came up with his own proposal. In his eyes, two solutions were possible: a negative tax or the "demogrants," which corresponds to a UBI. Tobin's preference was clearly for the second option, which does not create the same complications for those with less tax knowledge and a greater need for this subsidy. Read in particular James Tobin, Joseph A. Pechman and Peter M. Mieszkowski, "Is a Negative Income Tax Practical?," *The Yale Law Journal*, vol. 77, no. 1 (1967): 1–27. Also read the interview that Tobin gave to Philippe Van Parijs in 1998 that is found on BIEN's Web site: www.basicincome.org.
16. See Anthony Atkinson, "The Case for a Participation Income" in *The Political Quarterly*, vol. 67, no. 1 (1996): 67–70.
17. Read Bill Jordan, Phil Agulnik, Duncan Burbidge and Stuart Duffin, *Stumbling Towards Basic Income*, (London: Citizen's Income Study Centre, 2000).
18. The idea of instituting a modest allowance during a transition period raises a lot of opposition. Claudine Leleux, for example, says that "such 'symbolic' amounts seem to *discredit the idea even* of a BI in public opinion...." (trans.) She feels that a modest unconditional income would "fuel the belief that a UBI would serve to radically dismantle the social security system." (trans.) André Gorz goes even further: "A very low 'existence income' is, in fact, an employer's subsidy. It allows them to obtain work while paying below subsistence wages." (trans.) I naturally disagree with these points of view, which I believe reflect a misunderstanding of the distributive dynamic of a full or partial BI. See Claudine Leleux, *Travail ou revenu: Pour un revenu inconditionnel* (Paris: Éditions du Cerf, 1998), quotes found on pages 96 and 52 and André Gorz, *Misères du présent, richesse du possible* (Paris: Galilée, 1997), quote found on pages 136 to 137.
19. However, even a modest BI should have a positive effect on poverty since it would normally consititute a net gain for the working poor.
20. For an "improved version" of the MacDonald proposal, see Michael Wolfson, "A Guaranteed Income" in *Policy Options/Options Politiques* (January 1986): 35–45.
21. For a complete introduction scenario offering every Canadian an allowance of $5,000 ($7,000 for pensioners and $3,000 for children), see Sally Lerner, Charles Clark and Robert Needham, *Basic Income:*

Economic Security for All Canadians (Toronto: Between the Lines, 1999).

22. Read in particular pages 877 to 883 of the report (French version) to get an idea of the two options proposed by the Commission.
23. On this topic, see Robert Van der Veen and Loek Groot, eds., *Basic Income on the Agenda: Policy Options and Political Feasibility* (Amsterdam: Amsterdam University Press, 2000).
24. I think that a partial BI also responds to the objection made by Jon Elster. He states that changes brought about by a BI would be so great that they could not be anticipated by social science, at least as it is today. On this subject, see Jon Elster, "Comment on Van der Veen and Van Parijs," *Theory and Society*, vol. 15, no. 15 (1986): 709–721.
25. See Patrick O'Brien and Dennis Olson, "The Alaska permanent fund and dividend distribution program" in *Public Finance Quarterly*, vol. 18, no. 2 (1990): 139–156.
26. See Jean-Marc Ferry, *L'Allocation universelle. Pour un revenu de citoyenneté* (Paris: Cerf, 1995). For further reading on the topic, see Joseph Huber and James Robertson, *Creating New Money: A Monetary Reform of the Information Age* (London: New Economics Foundation, 2000).
27. On this particular strategy, read the important work of Edmund S. Phelps, *Rewarding Work* (Cambridge: Harvard University Press, 1997).
28. See Anthony B. Atkinson, *Poverty in Europe* (London: Blackwell, 1998), particularly pages 140–145.
29. In Canada, close to half of the tax expenditure for these programs goes to the wealthiest 10 per cent of taxpayers.
30. This is one of the conclusions drawn by Pierre Rosanvallon in *La Crise de l'État-providence* (Paris: Éditions du Seuil, 1981).
31. Today, in fact, democracy is certainly a required condition of justice but it cannot be a condition sufficient onto itself.
32. On this theme, read Bo Rothstein, "The Moral Logic of the Universal Welfare State," in Erik Oddvar Eriksen and Jørn Loftager, eds., *The Rationality of the Welfare State* (Oslo: Scandinavian University Press), 99–119.
33. See Hans-Werner Sinn, "Tax Harmonisation or Tax Competition in Europe?," *European Economic Review* 34 (1990): 489–504.
34. See in particular Jean-Marc Ferry, *L'Allocation universelle. Pour un revenu de citoyenneté* (Paris: Cerf, 1995) and Philippe Van Parijs, "Utopie pour le temps présent" in *Revue Agone*, no. 21 (1999): 91–104.

35. See Jan Tinbergen, *Reshaping the International Order: A Report to the Club of Rome* (New York: Dutton & Co., 1976); James E. Meade, *A Geometry of International Trade* (George Allen & Unwin, 1952). For a presentation of this proposal, read Myron J. Frankman, "Le revenu universel: un antidote à l'apartheid global," in *Revue Agone*, 21 (1999): 105–118.

Bibliography

ACKERMAN, Bruce and Anne ALSTOTT. *The Stakeholder Society*. New Haven: Yale University Press, 1999.
ANSPACH, Mark Rogin. "L'archipel du Welfare américain. Âge d'abondance, Âge de pierre." In *La Revue du MAUSS*, vol. 7, no. 1 (1996).
ATKINSON, Anthony B. *Poverty in Europe*. London: Blackwell, 1998.
———. "The Case for a Participation Income." In *The Political Quarterly*, vol. 67, no. 1 (1996): 67–70.
———. *Public Economics in Action: The Basic Income/Flat Tax*. Oxford: Oxford University Press, 1995.
BAECHLER, Jean. *Le Capitalisme*. Paris: Gallimard, 1995.
BARBIER, Jean-Claude and Jérôme Gautié (eds.). *Les Politiques de l'emploi en Europe et aux États-Unis*. Paris: Presses universitaires de France, 1998.
BARR, Nicholas. *The Economics of the Welfare State*. Stanford: Stanford University Press, 1993.
BARRY, Brian. *Theories of Justice*. Berkeley: University of California Press, 1989.
———. "Intergenerational Justice in Energy Policy." In Douglas Maclean and Peter G. Brown (eds.). *Energy and the Future*. Totowa: Rowman and Littlefield, 1983, 15–30.
BÉLANGER, Paul R. and Benoît LÉVESQUE. In "Le rapport Macdonald et le marché du travail." *Perception*, vol. 9, no. 3 (1986): 17–19.
BELLAMY, Edward. *Looking Backward*. Harmondsworth: Penguin Books, 1983 (1897).
———. *Equality*. New York: Appleton, 1897.
BERNARD, Michel and Michel CHARTRAND. *Manifeste pour un revenu de citoyenneté*. Montreal: Éditions du renouveau québécois, 1999.
BERTEN, André, Pablo DA SILVEIRA and Hervé POURTOIS. *Libéraux et communautariens*. Paris: Presses universitaires de France, 1997.
BESLEY, Timothy. "Means Testing versus Universal Provision in Poverty Alleviation." In *Economica* 57 (1990):119–129.
BLAIS, François. "Loisir, travail et réciprocité: une justification rawlsienne de l'allocation universelle est-elle possible?" In *Loisir et société/Soci-*

ety and Leisure, vol. 22, no. 2 (1999): 337–353.
BRESSON, Yoland. *Le Partage du temps et des revenus*. Paris: Economica, 1994.
BRITTAN, Samuel. *Capitalism with a Human Face*. Aldershot: Edward Elgar, 1995.
———. *Beyond the Welfare State: An Examination of Basic Income in a Market Economy*. London: Aberdeen University Press, 1990 (in collaboration with Steven Webb).
CAMERON, Duncan. "La commission Macdonald et l'autre rapport Macdonald." *Perception*, vol. 9, no. 1 (1985): 10–12.
CASTEL, Robert. *Les Métamorphoses de la question sociale. Une chronique du salariat*. Paris: Éditions de l'Atelier, 1997.
CHARLIER, Joseph. *La Question sociale résolue. Précédée du testament philosophique d'un penseur*. Bruxelles: P. Weissenbruch, 1894.
COLLECTIF CHARLES FOURIER. In *La Revue nouvelle*, vol. 81, no. 1 (April 1985): 345–360.
COMMISSION OF INQUIRY ON UNEMPLOYMENT INSURANCE. *Report*. Ottawa: Minister of Supply and Services, 1986.
DOUGLAS, Clifford H. *Economic Democracy*. Sudbury: Bloomfield, 1974 (1920).
———. *Social Credit*. London: Spottiswoode, 1934.
DUTIL, Robert. *La Juste Inégalité. Essai sur la liberté, l'égalité et la démocratie*. Montreal: Québec/Amérique, 1995.
DWORKIN, Ronald. "What is Equality? Part II: Equality of Resources." In *Philosophy and Public Affairs* 10 (1981): 283–345.
———. *Taking Rights Seriously*. London: Duckworth, 1977.
ELLWOOD, David T. *Poor Support: Poverty in the American Family*. New York: Basic Books, 1988.
ELSTER, Jon. "Is there (or should there be) a right to work?" In Amy Gutmann (ed.). *Democracy and the Welfare State*. Princeton: Princeton University Press, 1988, 53–78.
———. "Comment on Van der Veen and Van Parijs." *Theory and Society*, vol. 15, no. 15 (1986): 709–721.
ERIKSEN, Erik Oddvar and Jørn LOFTAGER (eds.). *The Rationality of the Welfare State*. Oslo: Scandinavian University Press, 1996.
FERRY, Jean-Marc. *L'Allocation universelle. Pour un revenu de citoyenneté*. Paris: Cerf, 1995.
FLEURBAEY, Marc. *Théories économiques de la justice*. Paris: Economica, 1996.
FITZPATRICK, Tony. *Freedom and Security: An Introduction to the Basic Income Debate*. London: Macmillan Press, 1999.

FORTIN, Bernard, Guy LACROIX and Jean-Yves DUCLOS. *L'Univers de l'aide sociale: les plus démunis peuvent-ils s'en sortir?* Social research. Conseil québécois de la recherche sociale, vol. 6, no. 1 (1999).

FOURIER, Charles. La Fausse Industrie, morcelée, répugnante, mensongère, et l'antidote, l'industrie naturelle, combinée, attrayante, véridique, donnant quadruple produit et perfection extrême en toutes qualités. Paris: Anthropos, 1967.

FRANKMAN, Myron J. "Le revenu universel: un antidote à l'apartheid global." *Revue Agone*, no. 21 (1999): 105–118.

FRIEDMAN, Milton. "The Case for the Negative Income Tax: a View from the Right." In J. H. Bunzel (ed.). *Issues of American Public Policy*. Englewood Cliffs: Prentice Hall, 1968/1966, 111–120.

———. *Capitalism and Freedom*. Chicago: University of Chicago Press, 1975 (1960).

FUNICIELLO, Theresa. *Tyranny of Kindness: Dismantling the Welfare System to End Poverty in America*. New York: Atlantic Monthly Press, 1993.

GAUTHIER, David. *Morals by Agreement*. Oxford: Clarendon Press, 1986.

GILAIN, Bruno and Philippe VAN PARIJS. "L'allocation universelle: un scénario de court terme et son impact distributif." *Revue belge de sécurité sociale* (1st quarter, 1996): 5–74.

GIRAUD, Pierre-Noël. *L'Inégalité du monde. Économie du monde contemporain*. Paris: Gallimard, 1996.

GODINO, Roger. "Réformer la fiscalité des revenus faibles en créant une Allocation Compensatrice de Revenu." In *La Lettre (Action pour le Renouveau Socialiste)* 84 (Paris: 2000).

———. "Pour la création d'une allocation compensatrice de revenu." In *Pour une réforme du RMI*. Paris: notes from the Fondation Saint-Simon, 1999.

GOODIN, Robert E. "Towards a Minimally Presumptuous Social Welfare Policy." In Philippe Van Parijs (ed.). *Arguing for Basic Income*. London: Verso, 1992, 195–214.

———. *Reasons for Welfare*. Princeton: Princeton University Press, 1988.

GORZ, André. *Misères du présent, richesse du possible*. Paris: Galilée, 1997.

———. *Métamorphoses du travail. Quête du sens et critique de la raison économique*. Paris: Galilée, 1988.

———. *Reclaiming Work: Beyond the Wage-Based Society*. Cambridge Malden: Polity Press/Blackwell, 1999.

GOVERNMENT OF QUEBEC, DEPARTMENT OF FINANCE. *Les Taux marginaux implicites de taxation*. Quebec, 1999.

GUEST, Dennis. *The Emergence of Social Security in Canada.* Vancouver: University of British Columbia Press, 1988 (c1985).

HUBER, Joseph and James ROBERTSON. *Creating New Money: A Monetary Reform of the Information Age.* London: New Economics Foundation, 2000.

HUMAN RESOURCES DEVELOPMENT CANADA. The Guaranteed Annual Income: an information paper. Ottawa: 1994.

JORDAN, Bill, Phil AGULNIK, Duncan BURBIDGE and Stuart DUFFIN. *Stumbling Towards Basic Income.* London: Citizen's Income Study Centre, 2000.

LARMORE, Charles. *Modernité et morale.* Paris: Presses universitaires de France, 1993.

La Revue du MAUSS. Vers un revenu minimum inconditionnel, vol. 7, no. 1 (1996).

LELEUX, Claudine. *Travail ou revenu? Pour un revenu inconditionnel.* Paris: Cerf, 1998.

LERNER, Sally, Charles CLARK and Robert NEEDHAM. *Basic Income: Economic Security for All Canadians.* Toronto: Between the Lines, 1999.

MEADE, James E. *Retour au plein-emploi?* Paris: Economica, 1996.

———. *A Geometry of International Trade.* George Allen & Unwin, 1952.

MÉDA, Dominique. "L'ambiguïté d'un revenu minimum inconditionnel." In *La Revue du MAUSS*, vol. 7, no. 1 (1996):169–173.

———. *Le Travail, une valeur en voie de disparition.* Paris: Aubier, 1995.

MILNER, Dennis. *Higher Production by a Bonus on National Output: A Proposal for a Minimum Income for All Varying with National Productivity.* London: George Allen & Unwin, 1920.

MOYNIHAN, Daniel. *The Politics of a Guaranteed Income: The Nixon Administration and the Family Assistance Plan.* New York: Random House, 1973.

NATIONAL COUNCIL OF WELFARE, *Poverty Profile 1995.* Ottawa: Ministry of Supply and Services, 1997.

OFFE, Claus. "Droits et ressources économiques du citoyen: Vers un nouvel équilibre?" In *Societal cohesion and the globalising economy.* Paris: Organization for Economic Co-operation and Development (OECD)1997, 91–121.

———. "Full Employment: Asking the Wrong Question." Erik Oddvar Eriksen and Jørn Loftager (eds.). *The Rationality of the Welfare State.* Oslo: Scandinavian University Press, 1996, 121–133.

O'BRIEN, Patrick and Dennis OLSON. "The Alaska permanent fund and dividend distribution program." In *Public Finance Quarterly*, vol. 18, no. 2 (1990): 139–56.

OKUN, Arthur M. *Equality and Efficiency: The Big Tradeoff.* Washington: The Brookings Institution, 1975.

ORGANIZATION FOR ECONOMIC CO-OPERATION AND DEVELOPMENT (OECD). *Making work pay: taxation, benefits, employment and unemployment.* Paris: 1997.

PAINE, Thomas. "Agrarian Justice." In *La Revue du MAUSS. Vers un revenu minimum inconditionnel*, vol. 7, no. 1 (1996): 23–36.

PARETO, Vilfredo. *Cours d'économie politique.* Geneva: Droz, 1964.

PARKER, Hermione. *Taxes, Benefit and Family Life: The Seven Deadly Traps.* London: Institute of Economic Affairs, 1995.

———. *Citizen's Income and Women.* Basic Income Research Group Discussion Paper, no. 2. London: Citizen Income Study Centre, 1993.

———. *Instead of the Dole: An Enquiry into Integration of the Tax and Benefit Systems.* London: Routledge, 1989.

PHELPS, Edmund S. *Rewarding Work: How to Restore Participation and Self-Support to Free Entreprise.* Cambridge: Harvard University Press, 1997.

PIKETTY, Thomas. *L'Économie des inégalités.* Paris: La Découverte, 1997.

POLANYI, Karl. *The Great Transformation.* Boston: Beacon Hill Press, 1958 (c1944). Paris: Gallimard, 1983.

RAWLS, John. *Political Liberalism.* New York: Columbia University Press, 1993.

———. *A Theory of Justice.* Cambridge: Belknap Press of Harvard University, 1971.

REYNOLDS, Brigid and Sean HEALY. *Towards an Adequate Income for All.* Conference of Religious of Ireland, 1994.

RHYS-WILLIAMS, Lady Juliet. *Something to Look Forward To.* London: Macdonald, 1943.

RIFKIN, Jeremy. *The End of Work: the Decline of the Global Labour Force and the Dawn of the Post-Market Era.* New York: G.P. Putnam's Sons, 1995.

ROBEYNS, Ingrid. "An Emancipation Fee or Hush Money? The advantages and disadvantages of a basic income for women's emancipation and well-being." Conference presented at the 7th International Convention of the Basic Income European Network, Amsterdam.

ROSANVALLON, Pierre. *La Nouvelle Question sociale. Repenser l'État-providence.* Paris: Seuil, 1995.

———. *La Crise de l'État-providence.* Paris: Éditions du Seuil, 1981.

ROTHSTEIN, Bo. "The Moral Logic of the Universal Welfare State." In

Erik Oddvar Eriksen and Jørn Loftager (eds.). *The Rationality of the Welfare State*. Oslo: Scandinavian University Press, 99–119.

ROYAL COMMISSION ON THE ECONOMIC UNION AND DEVELOPMENT PROSPECTS FOR CANADA. *Report*. Ottawa: Supply and Services Canada, 1985.

SAUNDERS, Peter. "Improving work incentitives in a means-tested welfare system: the 1994 Australian social security reforms." *Fiscal Studies*, vol. 16, no. 2 (1995): 45–70.

SEN, Amartya. *Inequality Reexamined*. New York/Cambridge: Russell Sage Foundation/Harvard University Press, 1992.

SINN, Hans-Werner. "Tax Harmonisation or Tax Competition in Europe?" European Economic Review 34 (1990): 489–504.

SIROIS, Charles. *Passage obligé. Passeport pour l'ère nouvelle*. Montreal: Les Éditions de l'Homme, 1999.

STANDING, Guy. *Global Labour Flexibility: Seeking Distributive Justice*. Basingstoke: Macmillan, 1999.

———. "Meshing labour flexibility with security: an answer to mass unemployment?" In *International Labour Review* 125 (1986): 87–106.

STEINER, Hillel. *An Essay on Rights*. Oxford: Blackwell, 1994.

———. "Three Just Taxes." In Philippe Van Parijs (ed.). *Arguing for Basic Income*. London and New York: Verso, 1992.

STIGLER, George. "The Economics of Minimum Wage Legislation." *American Economic Review* (1946): 358–365.

STOLERU, Lionel. *Vaincre la pauvreté dans les pays riches*. Paris: Flammarion, 1974.

THEOBALD, Robert (ed.). *The Guaranteed Income*. New York: Doubleday, 1966.

———. *Free Men and Free Markets*. New York: Anchor Books, 1965.

TINBERGEN, Jan. *Reshaping the International Order: A Report to the Club of Rome*. New York: Dutton & Co., 1976.

TITMUSS, Richard. "Universal and Selective Social Services." In Brian Abel-Smith and Kay Titmuss (eds.). *The Philosophy of Welfare: Selected Writings of Richard M. Titmuss*. London: Allen & Unwin, 1987, 128–140.

TOBIN, James, Joseph A. PECHMAN and Peter M. MIESZKOWSKI. "Is a Negative Income Tax Practical?" *The Yale Law Journal*, vol. 77, no. 1 (1967): 1–27.

VAILLANCOURT, Yves. *L'Évolution des politiques sociales au Canada et au Québec 1940–1960*. Montreal: Presses de l'Université de Montréal, 1988.

VAN DER VEEN, Robert and Loek GROOT (eds.). *Basic Income on the Agenda: Policy Options and Political Feasibility*. Amsterdam: Amsterdam University Press, 2000.

VAN DER VEEN, Robert J. and Philippe VAN PARIJS. "A Capitalist Road to Communism." In *Theory and Society*, vol. 15, no. 5 (1986): 635–656.

VAN PARIJS, Philippe. "Utopie pour le temps présent." In *Revue Agone* 21 (1999): 91–104.

———. *Refonder la solidarité*. Paris: Cerf, 1997.

———. "Du patrimoine naturel aux régimes de retraite." In *Refonder la solidarité*. Paris: Cerf, 1997, 67–95.

———. "De la trappe au socle, l'allocation universelle contre le chômage." *La Revue du MAUSS*, vol. 7, no.1 (1996): 90–104.

———. *Real Freedom for All*. Oxford: Clarendon Press, 1995.

———. *Sauver la solidarité*. Paris: Cerf, 1995.

———. (ed). *Arguing for Basic Income*. London and New York: Verso, 1992.

———. "La préhistoire du débat: l'ombre de Speenhamland." *La Revue nouvelle* 4 (1985): 395–399.

VAN TRIER, Walter. *Every One A King*. Doctorat disseration. Louvain Catholic University: Sociology Department, 1995.

WALTER, Tony. *Basic Income: Freedom from Poverty, Freedom to Work*. London and New York: Marion Boyar, 1989.

WELLMAN, Carl. *Welfare Rights*. Totowa: Rowman and Littlefield, 1982.

WHITE, Stuart. "Liberal equality, exploitation and the case for an unconditional basic income." In *Political Studies* 45 (1997): 312–326.

WOLFSON, Michael. "A Guaranteed Income." In *Policy Options/Options politiques*. (January 1986): 35–45.

WOOD, Adrian. *North-South Trade, Employment and Inequality*. Oxford: Oxford University Press, 1994.

Index

academic trap, 89–90
Aid to Families with Dependent Children, 4
AIRE, 103
Alaska, 86
annuity incomes, 93
anti-poverty movement, 18–19, 61
Aristotle, 49
assets (personal), 51–52
Association pour l'instauration d'un revenu d'existence (AIRE), 103
autonomy, 18, 87

Basic Grant, 5
Basic Income: administration, 38–39; alternatives to, 86–88; costs, 67–69, 86; criticism, 112n, xvi; defenders, xvi; definition, 1; economic grounds for, 37–48; global, 99–100; history, 1–2; ideal level, 58, 62; implementation of, 65, 77, 86, 79–94; indexing, 88–89; and need, 71–74; other terms for, 3–5; paradox, 62; self-financing, 70–71; support, 2–3, 37–38, 111n
Basic Income/Canada, 103–104
Basic Income European Network (BIEN), 103, 108n
benefits, 30, 59, 64; and GNP, 31–32, 10; and taxes, 16–17
Beveridge Plan, 33–34
BIEN, 103, 108n
budgetary cost, 66–67
budgetary effort, 69–70
bureaucracy, 40–41, 74

capitalism, 32, 63
cash benefits, 59
Citizen's Income, 5
Citizen's Income Study Centre, 104
citizenship, 51
Citizenship, Income and Society Webring, 105
coercive power, 95
cohabitation, 75, 83
collective wealth, 23, 52–53, 88–89, 100
community, 50, 55, 76
compassion, 96–97
competition, 28–29; *see also* globalization; markets
conditional assistance programs, 2–3, 4, 6, 40–41
cost of living, 88–89
creative activities, 50
culture of poverty, 14–15
cumulative rule, 6, 71, 71–72
cut-offs (income), 9–10, 58
democracy, 25, 29–30, 95, 96–97
dependency, 66, 82
dignity, 53–54, 55, 58
direct benefits, 64
direct marginal tax rates, 84–85; *see also* taxes
discrimination, 87
distribution (redistribution), 19, 28, 31, 80
distributive justice, 24
division of labour, 27
Douglas, Major Clifford H., 4

Earned Income Tax Credit, 43

economic justice, 25
economic partnerships, 99
economy: development, 21, 61; efficiency, 23–25; justice, 25; recovery of, 87; social policies, 28–33; sustainability, 60–61
education, 30–31, 90
effective tax rates, 13, 15, 38; *see also* taxes
efficiency, 21–23, 23–25, 28, 62–63
efficient redistribution, 28
egalitarianism, 59–60
ego, 95
employers, 46
employment, 13, 41–42, 55–58; job creation, 21, 87; demand for jobs, 32–33; income, 82–83; and inequality, 57–58; insurance, 90, 90–92; job sharing, 87; poorly paid, 42–43
employment insurance, 90, 90–92; *see also* social insurance
environmental protection, 61–62
environmentalists, 108n
equality/inequality, 26–27, 95, 96; employment, 57–58; and freedom, 25–26; material, 27–28; and social assistance, 90; wages, 92–93
ethics. *See* morality
European Basic Income, 100
exclusion: employment, 55–57; and poverty, xvii; workforce, 32
external assets, 52–53

fairness, 27–28; and efficiency, 24; and social insurance, 94. *See also* justice
federal responsibility, 85
financial security, 32–33
Forget Commission on Unemployment Insurance, 64–65
Fourier, Charles, 4
freedom(s), 55, 59–60; fundamental, 27–28; individual, 25, 27–28; and justice, 25
freedom of choice rule, 6, 59, 71, 75, 84

Friedman, Milton, 72, 113n
Future Work, 104

globalization, 37, 97–98, 99
goods and services production, 30, 32
government: collaboration, 85–88; and economic interventions, 28–29; and fiscal sovereignty, 97–98
grants, 89–90
Great Depression, 34
gross national product (GNP), 31, 87, 88
Guaranteed Annual Income, 3–4
Guaranteed Income Supplement, 72

health care, 17, 31, 41, 96
households: cost to, 66–67; earnings, 14, 78; shared, 83

impartiality, 95
income: household, 14; and net decreases, 84–85; participation, 76; security, 31–33, 91; and work, 18
income effect, 69, 102, 110n
Income Support, 4
income support programs. *See* social assistance
indexing: the BI, 88–89; minimum wage, 11
indirect benefits, 64
individualization, 14, 67–68, 74–75
individualization rule, 6, 71
inequality. *See* equality
insurance. *See* social insurance
internal assets, 52–53
international cooperation, 98
interventionism, 28–29

jobs. *See* employment
justice, 21–23, 53–54, 58–59, 94–95; corrective, 49; and democracy, 96–97; and distribution of wealth, 24, 60–61; and efficiency, 22–23, 62–63; meaning of, 24–25; social, 20, 48–62, 95; and wages, 45

Kant, Immanuel, 95
Keynesian economics: and social reform, 34

labour: division of, 27, 35; laws, 45; re-entry into l. market, 16, 19–20
"last resort assistance", 6
laziness, 50, 51; *see also* morality
low-income cut-offs, 9–10, 58
low-wage policies: and productivity, 47

MacDonald Commission, 64–65, 74, 79, 80–81, 85
marginal tax rates, 13, 15, 17, 72, 75, 78–79, 82; definition, 106
markets: competition, 28–29; opening, 36–37, 44
Marsh, Leonard, 34
minimex, 4
minimum wage, 9, 11–12, 44–45
moonlighting, 82
morality, 48–49, 51–52

negative income tax, 72–73, 73–74, 97, 102
"new economy", 36–37, 57–58
non-workers: 7–8, 10, 16, 18–19; definition, 106

Old Age Security, 93
opportunity: inequality of, 52–53
Organisation Advocating Support Income in Australia, 104

Paine, Thomas, 4, 53, 108n
Parti socialiste, 72
partial allowance, 77–79, 85
participation income, 76
pension plans, 90, 92–93
personal income tax, 74
personal tax credit, 80
poverty: combating, 15; culture of, 14–15; in industrialized nations, 7–9; lack of definition, 61; and minimum wage, 9; perceptions of, 7–8, xvii; traps, 12–15, 37, 68–69, 91;

private social insurance, 34
privileges, 25; *see also* freedom(s)
productivity: and BI, 46–48; and technology, 35–36
provincial responsibility, 85
pure redistribution, 28

"quaternary-sector" activities, 43
Quebec, 67–68

reciprocity, 49–51, 115n
redistribution of wealth, 19, 31
regressive social policies, 106
regulations, 30, 45
repayment (benefits), 16–17
retirement, 92–93
revenu minimum d'insertion, 4
"right to work" (and variations), 55–58
rights, 53; *see also* freedom(s)

salaries, 45–47; *see also* wages
security, 31–33, 93
self-esteem, 55
seniors, 72, 93
single mothers, 14; *see also* women
social assistance: administration, 38–39; compared to BI, 6; and conditionality, 6; dependency, 8; and employment, 41–42; quitting, 82–83; recipients, 2–3; replacing, 65–66, 77–79; and selectivity, 54; stigma of, 2–3, 63, 97; and taxes, 39–40
Social Credit Party, 4–5
social democracy, 29–30
Social Dividend, 4–5
social insurance, 34–35, 90–92, 111n; and poverty traps, 37
social justice, 20, 48–62, 95
social partnership, 50, 51, 90, 94–101
socialism, 117n
solidarity, 95
sovereignty (fiscal), 97–98
student loans, 89–90
subsidies, 87
supply and demand, 32

taste: and justice, 24–25
tax base, 76–77
taxes, 15, 16–17, 73, 94; credits, 80; deductions, 92–93; income from, 70; and redistribution, 39–40, 80, 81; and non-workers, 69
technology, 44; and labour, 46–47; and productivity, 35–36
Tobin, James, 120n
training, 47–48, 75, 88, 89–90
transparency, 39–40, 87; 99-100, 100

UBINZ, 104
unconditionality, 1, 4, 5–7, 49–51, 54
unemployment: involuntary, 91; traps, 12–15, 15–16, 91; *see also* employment
unions, 2, 65
United States: employment, 43; poverty, 7
Universal Basic Income, 5; *see also* Basic Income
Universal Basic Income New Zealand (UBINZ), 104
universality, 5, 38–39, 95
usefulness, 75–76

values, 51–52; and employment, 55; and reciprocity, 50; social, 22; *see also* morality
Vereniging Basisinkomen, 105
wages, 92–93
wealth. *See* collective wealth
welfare state, 59, 78–79; contemporary, 30, 32, 33–37; criticism of, 33, 37, 95; failures of, 35–36; reform, xiv; schemes, 8, 67-68
women: and BI, 2, 119n; in workforce, 35, 36, 43
work, 55–58; hours, 87; incentive, 42, 71; requirement, 75; and taxes, 15
workers, 8–9, 17–18: definition, 106; and net income, 83–84
workfare, 2–3, 15–16, 54, 106
workforce exclusion, 32

workhouses, 16
working poor. *See* workers
worth, 25–27

youth, 2, 14